APPALACHIAN GHOST STORIES AND OTHER TALES

JAMES GAY JONES

Professor of History
Glenville State College

McCLAIN PRINTING COMPANY
PARSONS, WEST VIRGINIA 26287

1975

Standard Book Number 87012-203-7
Library of Congress Card Number 74-24611
Printed in the United States of America
Copyright © 1975 by James Gay Jones
Glenville, West Virginia
All Rights Reserved

FIRST PRINTING 1975
SECOND PRINTING 1975
THIRD PRINTING 1977
FOURTH PRINTING 1980
FIFTH PRINTING 1983
SIXTH PRINTING 1990
SEVENTH PRINTING 1992
EIGHTH PRINTING 1992
NINTH PRINTING 1995

Preface

It was the custom in the days of my youth for somewhat isolated rural families to provide their social entertainment through long winter evenings by relating tales of ghosts, murders, legends and other folklore. From my parents and from visiting relatives and friends came some of the tales recounted here. Also, over a considerable period of time spent in the teaching profession, countless other tales have come to my attention through some of my more curious-minded students. For all those generous contributions I owe a considerable debt of gratitude.

This little volume consists of a limited selection of tales from the great variety of folklore extant in Appalachia. Because some of them were initially related to me in a more or less fragmentary form, I have taken the liberty to expand and develop those into what, I hope, are more engaging presentations. In those instances where the tale has appeared in a number of versions, both orally and in the printed form, I have attempted to choose those elements which, to me, appeared to be the most logical whenever logic was applicable. In the true experience stories where the use of correct names might bring embarrassment to someone, fictitious names have been substituted. Likewise, in those tales where the true names of participants have been forgotten or are unknown and there is a need to identify the characters involved, fictitious names have been used. Also, in cases where the event was claimed to have occurred in more than one place, an arbitrary selection of location has been made.

A few of these tales initially appeared in CONFRONTATION, a publication of the Learning Materials Center in the Robert F. Kidd Library of Glenville State College. In the preparation of those particular stories for inclusion here, some have been given new titles.

To those persons who have encouraged me to begin a compilation of these tales for publication, I wish to express my gratitude for their support; for without it, I feel sure, it would never have been started. Also, I am especially grateful for the help of my daughter, Kimberly, who gave indispensable aid in manuscript preparation.

J. G. J.

Glenville, W.Va.
October, 1974

Contents

Introduction

The rugged mountains and shadowy valleys of the Allegheny Highlands have been an ideal place for the creation and preservation of folklore. Many of the characteristics of the American frontier experience lingered here in some of the more remote areas into the early twentieth century. Because of poor means of transportation and communication, these dwellers in the isolated uplands experienced an arrested development that saw generations come and go with practically no change in their way of living.

In the movement of the American people westward through the Appalachian Highland, the most attractive avenues of migration -- the Potomac-Ohio and the Great Valley of Virginia -- led the great majority of the pioneers away from West Virginia. Some of the overflow penetrated the Alleghenies, but many of those sturdy yeomen who intended to settle there, on learning of the conflict in land claims, moved on to areas where land titles were more secure. Those who decided to stay faced a situation where literally millions of acres of Western Virginia land were controlled through absentee ownership. Moreover, this situation not only restricted the number of people who could find title-free homesteads in the region, but later permitted an easy and arrogant exploitation of the natural resources of those holdings in the late nineteenth and twentieth centuries. This factor, among others, had a bearing on the formation of the character of these people.

The isolated situation of the area as well as the severely limited means of communication among the people within precluded any substantive changes in their way of living, but instead, fostered a zealous particularism. Even after a number of so-called turnpikes were extended through the Alleghenies to the Ohio River, there were times when it was practically impossible to travel over them. Illustrative of this situation is a record of communication that arose as a result of the heavy snow storms during the winter of 1856. The Trotter Brothers of Staunton, Virginia, who held the contract for delivering the mail over the Staunton to Parkersburg Turnpike, were, on a number of occasions, reported to the Postmaster General in Washington for irregular service. On their receipt of a note of reprimand from a postal official, their reply was: "If you knock the gable end of Hell out and back it up against Cheat Mountain and rain fire and brimstone for forty days and forty nights, it won't melt the snow enough to get your damned mail through on time."

The people's loyalty and defense of their particular communities against all others is a factor that has been thoroughly ingrained in their heritage; moreover, it continues to this day as a factor in the defeat of efforts directed toward achieving united action among the people of adjoining communities. A remark once made by Eli "Rimfire" Hamrick may be cited as an example of an expression of particularism. Rimfire was a widely known hunter and guide who often directed distinguished people on hunting trips into the mountains. Once, as an act of appreciation for his services as a guide, he was taken on a sight-seeing tour of New York City, which was his first trip outside his home state. When, on his return home, he was asked what he thought of that city, he replied: "I don't think it'll ever 'mount to much 'cause it's too fer away."

Another factor of influence in the heritage of these Appalachian people was the course of their adjustment to a statutory code of law and order. There were times during the development of this frontier when neither law nor gospel was observed. A circuit rider, on his return to Eastern Virginia from a trip through parts of Southern Appalachia reported that "ninety-eight people out of every hundred in that God-forsaken country don't know when Sunday comes." Excessive drinking, cursing and brawling were common and occasional hand-to-hand fighting often ended with the participants maimed or killed. Concerning this form of fighting, Philip Doddridge, a frontier historian, wrote: "Although no weapons were used, fists, teeth, and feet were employed at will; but above all, the detestable practice of gouging, by which eyes were sometimes put out, rendered this mode of fighting frightful indeed."

Because of a lack of respect for law and morality by many people on this frontier, the State of Virginia not only tolerated the continuation of many of her old barbarous laws of colonial times, but proceeded to enact additional statutes of similar nature. One law stated that "for any person who steals a hog, shoat or pig, the penalty for the first offense is thirty-five lashes on the bare back or a fine of thirty dollars (in addition to eight dollars for the owner of the animal stolen); for the second offense, the penalty is two hours in a pillory on a public court day at the court house, and both ears nailed to the pillory for two hours (no exception made for women); for the third offense the penalty is death." In 1803, a man at Clarksburg was sentenced to be hanged for stealing. Also at Clarksburg, another man was convicted of having stolen an axe, a hat and a pair of stockings, at which time the court ordered "That the sheriff immediately tie the prisoner to the public whipping post and give him thirty lashes well laid on and deliver him to David Hughes, Constable, who shall deliver him to the next constable and so on until he shall be conveyed out of the county."

Persons found guilty of profanity, drunkenness and working on Sunday were usually fined. If unable to pay a fine, they were either put in the pillory or tied to the whipping post for punishment. In 1795, Sheriff John Prunty of Harrison County was fined for swearing twenty-two times in the presence of the court and the justice of the peace and was fined eighty-three cents for each oath. An account of the proceedings shows that the court "ordered that the said John Prunty be confined in the stocks for the space of five minutes . . . for his Damming the Court and the attorney who was there supporting the client's claim and the whole bunch. The Court and the attorney was D——d fools and a set of D——d scoundrels." The record further indicates that after being released, Prunty again showed disrespect and was confined for the remainder of the day.

For a number of felonious offenses the accused would sometimes be granted "benefit of clergy" after which he would be burned in the hand and then whipped at the whipping post. However, "benefit of clergy" could not be claimed in cases of first degree murder, knowingly possessing counterfeit money, burglary, the burning of the court house or the clerk's office, or felonious stealing from a church or meeting house. In some instances, however, it was possible to substitute a milder punishment for the death penalty after the establishment of a state penitentiary.

Many of these laws remained on the statute books of

Virginia until the middle of the nineteenth century. The support of such laws by the citizens varied with the occasion and the needs of the time. In this, and other ways, these stalwart, sometimes earthy, sometimes boisterous mountain people, through generations of endeavor, tamed a frontier and also, in the same process, tamed themselves. In their conquest of the Alleghenies, they who struggled to make it habitable also implanted and preserved ethical and religious values, the concepts of equality and freedom and a sincere respect for their heritage. Because they lived apart from the main currents of the national change, these people preserved a culture that is unique in American society.

In this climate of isolation, want of knowledge, superstition, and respect for tradition, folklore in its various forms flourished. The stories, in prose and in song, that were passed from generation to generation, constituted an important part of the culture of this frontier. Some of these stories had been brought in by settlers in practically the same form in which they originated in the Old Country and were preserved here through the decades with little or no change. Out of their own experiences came a myriad of tales: legends and stories concerning the heroic struggle they had with the Indians as well as with their inhospitable environment; tales about the misfortunes of pack peddlers; about roaming bands of horse-trading and fortune-telling gypsies; about itinerant tramps and beggars; about the tragic Civil War which broke the fireside circle in many homes; about ghosts, witches, murder, the occult and reincarnation; and tall tales which generally abounded in abundant detail and pioneer exaggeration.

The listener usually accepted the tall tale as a form of entertainment and little else. However, those tales which involved ghosts, witchcraft, murder, and the occult he did not

5

take so lightly. There was widespread belief, in those early times on the frontier, that witches were responsible for strange and incurable diseases and for unusual and unexplainable occurrences in the community. Just as the people often looked after their ailments in the absence of doctors, likewise they found ways to deal with witchcraft when without the benefit of priestly exorcism.

One method commonly used in dealing with witches was to draw a picture of the witch on a board or a tree and then shoot the picture with a silver bullet. This was supposed to place the witch under a spell which could be removed only by her borrowing something from the person afflicted by her enchantment. As a result, in many communities there were old women accused of witchcraft who would not be able to borrow anything from their neighbors. Such persons often became the subject of numerous tales.

For some of these people, support for their belief in witchcraft and demonology came, in part, from their religious training. Although these mountain people were often accustomed to violence, they, by and large, were a religious folk. Numerous religious affiliations, in which Protestant evangelical churches claimed the vast majority of the population, were organized throughout the region and from which came established patterns of behavior of enduring significance.

Their general regard for freedom extended as well to their religious practices. Many of these people were direct descendants of dissenters from established churches in the Old Country. Because of that heritage and their limited communication with others, literally hundreds of churches were organized in Southern Appalachia under local concepts of what ritual and dogma should be observed. Among others, the concepts of fundamentalism and literal interpretation of the Scriptures were, and continue to be, basic tenets of the belief of the members of these particular churches. Through this literal interpretation of the Bible came such practices as snake-handling, sipping of poison, speaking in tongues, the laying on of hands, and a belief in demons and witches.

Certain elements in the practice of frontier medicine were not far removed from witchcraft, magic and demonology. Because of a scarcity of professionally trained doctors, most people on this frontier, in time of illness, had to depend on home remedies which had been handed down to them from earlier generations. Perhaps some of those remedies could be traced to the old custom of brewing up potions for various witchcraft and sorcery practices.

Since, in most cases, these people did not know the causes of their illnesses, they often tried a number of known remedies and, in times of desperation, concocted new ones. They had learned through experience that tonics and teas made from herbs, roots, and tree bark were effective in curing certain diseases without their knowing why.

Yet intermixed with their rational remedies were others which were, partly or wholly, based upon magic. One special kind of tonic was made from the bark of seven different kinds of trees which was thought to possess magical curative powers. It was also believed that persons who were born after their fathers had died, as well as seventh sons of seventh sons, possessed magical powers for healing persons afflicted with thrash and mouth sores. As a way to stop excessive bleeding, it was suggested that the bleeding person's name be said three times, then read aloud verse six of the sixteenth chapter of Ezekiel, with the whole procedure to be repeated twice more. To get relief from toothache, the sufferer was advised to walk backward as many steps as the number of years of his age with a dead horse's jaw-bone in his mouth.

Many frontier doctors never had any formal medical schooling but were largely self-trained. Some of them, from their limited experience, endeavored to educate the people in the area of their ailments and how to cope with them. An example was one Dr. Gunn whose book, GUNN'S DOMESTIC MEDICINE, was published in 1832. By way of introduction he stated:"'I am writing a book not for the learned but for the unlearned." He stressed the bleeding of patients for "mortification and most other illnesses, the bleeding to continue until the patient no longer feels any pain." Concerning lockjaw, he wrote: "I have never heard of, nor seen the practice, but should a case of locked jaw occur in my practice, I would try the effect of a strong warm bath made of lye."

As for amputations, Dr. Gunn wrote: "Anyone can perform them unless he be an idiot or an absolute fool." He further stated that all the instruments needed to perform an amputation could be picked up around the home. "Then," he added, "with as many as may be necessary to hold the patient, you proceed."

Dr. Gunn, as well as many other doctors of his time, favored the treatment of patients suffering from boils or carbuncles with issues. Dr. Gunn described an issue as "an ulcer or sore formed by an artificial means." He further explained: "When you want what is called the pea or pepper issue, you make an incision large enough to admit one or more peas or grains of pepper, or anything else that will keep the sore draining." One critic of Dr. Gunn's treatment by the issue method wrote: "The idea of an issue seemed to be that if you had a boil or sore on one end of you, an issue is made on the other end of you so you can't decide which is worse and you sort of forget the whole thing." The fact that Dr. Gunn was a living example of good health during most of his ninety-two years belied the primitive concepts he held about the practice of medicine.

The stories these mountain people related about witches, ghosts, demons, and even tall tales, in a majority of cases, emanated from, or were built around, their rich legacy of true experiences. A study of the sources of true experience stories reveals that, in general, they are reminiscences of the past in association with such concomitant influences as hearsay, gossip, rumor and personal experiences of the relator. Also dreams, auditory and optical illusions and various psychological phenomena often contribute to their development, especially in ghost and horror tales which touch on fateful and mysterious tragedies.

Over the years most of these stories passed from generation to generation in the oral tradition. There are some folklorists today who decry any departure from that practice because, they aver, the oral form of expression has certain interpretative powers which cannot be expressed through the written word. There are others, however, who claim that to attempt to preserve it in its original pure state is futile because folklore, in much the same way as the rest of culture in this rapidly expanding communication era, is constantly changing.

Folklore has survived over the years because it served a purpose for those who preserved it. The people sang songs and related tales as an activity to attain the ends of social adjustment as well as a means of voicing their praise or protest. They created a medium of expression of immeasurable entertainment value for themselves which, at the same time, bound the people more closely together. It was their past which lived for them over and over again.

9

Cale Betts' Ghost

About three miles below Grantsville in the Little Kanawha River Valley is a place once known as the Cale Betts farm. Shortly after Cale Betts disappeared, a ghost came to the farm home which led the members of the family to suspect that Cale had been murdered and that this was his ghost. The subsequent events that occurred thereabouts became so notorious that national attention was directed to the place through the newspapers of that time. Apart from the news media, there has been a considerable amount of oral information about the ghost that has passed from generation to generation to this day in that area of the valley.

The rambunctious ghost became so disturbing to the Betts family that Cale's son, Collins, decided to build a new house at another place on the farm. Just as soon as that house was completed, the family moved into it and then tore down the old house. Thereafter, the Betts family lived undisturbed in their new home.

Sometime after the old house had been razed, the ghost moved to the home of a farmer who lived nearby. Members of this family, at times, became disturbed when they felt a light breeze as the invisible ghost moved past them. The children were often frightened when the ghost, either inadvertently or purposely, tripped them while they played about their home. All sorts of noises were heard in and about the house at night none of which could be logically explained.

10

Although the farmer always barred the doors at night, they were often found open when morning came. Even when there was not the slightest wind blowing on one occasion, the lights were blown out as fast as they could be relit. These unexplainable happenings so frightened the family that to continue to live there became untenable. As soon as another house at the other end of the farm could be made ready, the family moved into it. In doing so, not only their former well-kept farm house was deserted, but the garden, the orchard and other possessions of the family at the old homestead were completely abandoned.

It is believed the ghost must have become lonesome when it found itself alone in the old farmhouse because it soon thereafter made its appearance at the nearest highway where it apparently tried to communicate with passersby. However, for some time, its efforts seemed to be fruitless and only frightened those who saw it.

On one occasion some boys suddenly came upon the ghost and began to throw stones at it. When they saw that the stones went through the ghost without affecting it, they fled in terror.

When young Tom Vandevener was riding in his wagon along the road one night about a half-mile from the Betts farm, his thoughts were far away from his immediate sur-roundings. Only a pale moonlight filtered through the clouds, yet visibility was sufficient for keeping in the roadway with-out undue difficulty. After a time Tom became aware of what he thought was a man walking in the road just ahead of his horses. For some distance they traveled in this manner with the man seemingly unaware of the nearness of the horses to him. When Tom tightened on the reins to slacken the pace of the horses, the phantom man glided without any noise back past the horses, climbed into the wagon and sat

11

down on the seat beside Tom.

To state that Tom did not cry out or run does not mean he was not afraid. The truth is he was so scared he could not move or even speak. In that condition he rode along with the ghost for several hundred yards. He was afraid to look directly at the ghost but through the corner of his eye it appeared to him to be headless; yet it talked to him. It told him not to be afraid for it would not harm him. Also, it warned him not to say anything about his seeing it until the old moon had gone out and a new moon had come in. Then it glided noiselessly off the wagon and disappeared into the woods.

Many people thereabouts believed, as the members of the Betts family did, that Cale Betts had been murdered. Moreover, they regarded the appearance of the ghost as his uneasy spirit seeking retribution for the crime.

Wizard's Clip and the Exorcist

In 1790 Adam Livingston moved his family from Pennsylvania to a seventy-five acre farm adjoining the village of Middleway in Jefferson County, Virginia (now West Virginia). About four years after settling there, a middle-aged stranger came and asked for board and lodging in the Livingston home. Since only two of the seven Livingston children were living at home at the time, it was thought there would be ample room for the stranger and he was permitted to stay.

Only a few days after the arrival of the stranger, he became ill. When his condition became worse, he called Adam to his bedside, informed him he was a Roman Catholic and asked if there was a priest in the neighborhood. Thereupon Adam, who was an intensely bigoted member of the Lutheran Church, replied that he knew of none and, even if there were any, he would never knowingly permit a Catholic priest to cross the threshold of his house. When the stranger realized he was going to die, he pleaded desperately for spiritual solace, but Adam turned a deaf ear and allowed the man to die without the comforting aid of a priest.

Following the death of the stranger, Adam employed Jacob Foster, a young man of the community, to sit up with the corpse through the night. When darkness approached, some new candles were brought in and lit. These candles, however, would not burn; as fast as they were lit, the fire flickered momentarily and then died out. Thinking their

13

newness prevented them from burning properly, Adam brought in two older candles from his own room and which had already burned about a third down. These were lit and placed on tables on opposite sides of the room, but immediately flickered out and left the room in darkness. Foster now became so frightened he ran out of the house and never returned. So Adam had to keep the wake with the corpse of the stranger.

The next night after the burial of the stranger, Adam was awakened by a noise that sounded like horses galloping round his house. He arose and went to a window to see what the commotion might be. He looked out into the bright moonlit night, but there were no horses to be seen.

In the days that immediately followed this incident, there came a series of misfortunes to Adam Livingston. It was a time of such confusion that, of all the narrators of the events of that time, it appears that no two have presented them in the same order of occurrence. Perhaps Adam, himself, in his time of troubles, did not remember the time order in which they came. Nevertheless, there was the report that crockeryware jumped off the tables and broke on the floor; a huge rope closed off the road in front of the house and then just as mysteriously disappeared; all his money was taken away; his barn burned and all his cattle died; and coals of fire jumped out of the fireplace and danced about on the floor.

Throughout this time, Adam was greatly annoyed but seemed to meet these apparent tricks of witchery with stoic fortitude. But when the chilling clip of the wizard's scissors came, he was terrified. First, the heads of Mrs. Livingston's turkeys, chickens and ducks were clipped off. Then the clipping of the shears could be heard in the various rooms of the Livingston house. Within a period of two or three weeks, the scissors had clipped half-moons and other curious-shaped designs in the blankets, counterpanes, sheets, clothing and draperies; even Adam's boots and saddles did not escape the wizard's shears.

Word of the strange occurrences at the Livingston homestead soon spread much beyond the village of Middleway. An elderly lady of Martinsburg heard about it and, to satisfy her curiosity, decided to visit the Livingstons and see for herself.

On her arrival at the Livingston homestead and before leaving her carriage, she removed her black cap, folded it neatly in a silk handkerchief and placed it in her pocket so it would not be clipped by the wizard's scissors. Then she went inside the house.

After visiting there for about a half-hour, she came out and entered her carriage to return home. When she removed the handkerchief from her pocket and unfolded it, she found her silk cap cut into narrow ribbons.

Three brash young men of Winchester, on hearing the strange tales being circulated about the wizard, announced they did not believe such reports and would prove them baseless if given an opportunity. On their arrival at the Livingston home they explained their mission and were graciously invited to spend the night there.

That night while the three men sat in the livingroom and made trite remarks about people who believed in wizardry, a large stone came out of the fireplace and, with great speed, whizzed about the room. In terror, the men fled from the house; they could hardly believe they had escaped from such a hazard without being harmed. Their sudden departure for Winchester indicated they had no further desire to question the presence of the wizard.

The mental torture that Adam Livingston suffered day and night without any relief brought him to the verge of nervous exhaustion. Now desperately seeking help, he had three self-styled "conjurers" to come and try to get the wizard out of the house, but they failed.

During one night of fitful sleeping, Adam dreamed of climbing a high mountain. On reaching the mountain top, he saw a person dressed in a black robe standing there. As he gazed upon the man, he heard a voice say: "This is the one who can save you."

When Adam awoke, he still recalled the dream in vivid detail; yet he was adamant about not having a Catholic priest in his house. Then the thought came to him that the black-robed person in his dream could have represented a minister of the Protestant faith. He knew an Episcopal minister who wore a robe in his church services, so he went to him for help. That minister, however, told Adam he could not help him.

Finally, Adam came to the conclusion he would have to see a Catholic priest to get relief from his troubles. At that time in Leetown, a village only a few miles east of Middleway, there lived the McSherry family who were of the Roman Catholic faith. To them Adam went seeking the whereabouts of a priest. Mrs. McSherry informed him that the Reverend Dennis Cahill would be at the Catholic Church in Shepherdstown on the following Sunday.

When Sunday came, Adam arose early and rode over to Shepherdstown. He soon located the Catholic Church, entered and sat down in a pew near the door. When the priest came out to the altar, tears came to Adam's eyes as he whispered audibly: "That is the man I saw in my dream; I'm sure he can help me!"

When the church service was over, Adam met the Reverend Cahill and explained his situation to him. Thereupon the priest accompanied Adam back to Middleway. The priest's first act on arriving there was to sprinkle holy water throughout the interior of Adam's house. Soon thereafter, Adam's money, which had disappeared earlier, was returned to the front doorsill. The clipping noise, however, continued. The priest next suggested that mass be celebrated in the house. At the conclusion of the mass, the clipping sound stopped. Never again did the wizard disturb the Livingston home. Because of these strange occurrences, the village of Middleway was known for over a half-century afterward as Wizard Clip and Cliptown.

Suffer Not a Witch to Live

Jim Bonner's farm was widely known as one of the best in the whole Little Kanawha River Valley. It consisted mostly of rich bottom land none of which, as far as anyone could recall, had ever been under water with the highest of floods in the river. Through good farming practices the Bonners grew in wealth and lived with considerable affluence in their community.

On the hill back of the Bonner farm lived Jake Spittle and his wife, Vergie, on a rocky, sub-marginal farm from which they barely eked out an existence. Neither inheritance nor environment had been kind to Vergie. Her reddish, scraggly hair, beady dark eyes, high cheek bones and long aquiline nose made her grossly unattractive. Moreover, her custom of wearing her husband's old slouch hat and rubbing snuff with a spicewood twig only added to her grotesque appearance and earned for her the name of "Vergie the Witch."

The first evidence of any unusual developments in the relations of the two families came after a dispute over a request by the Spittles for a right-of-way through the Bonner farm. They wanted to exchange a part of their farm for a strip of land to the river, but the Bonners refused. A short time after this when the two Bonner boys were passing through the Spittle farm, Vergie confronted them and threatened to put a hex on them if they were ever caught on her farm again. The boys reported the threat to their mother

18

who, not wanting to take any chances, promptly sewed a buckeye in a pocket of each of the boys' trousers to protect them from the evil eye of Vergie.

From this point on a number of inconveniences began to affect the Bonner household. First the milk suddenly became blink; then blood appeared in the eggs; and soon thereafter three pigs choked to death because their breathing passages became clogged with grubs. Although these were not entirely new experiences, it did seem unusual to the Bonners that they came so soon after Vergie had made known her possession of the hex power.

Grandpa Bonner, who had received a leg wound in the Civil War, spent much of his time at the Bonner home in his favorite rocking chair on the front porch and whiled away the time by reading his Bible, swatting flies and cat-napping. One day when one of the Bonner boys was suffering from a painful toothache, Grandpa pointed out to his ailing grandson a tree that had been struck by lightning and asked him to get a piece of limb that had been severed from the tree. As soon as the boy returned with the limb, Grandpa extracted a splinter with which he rubbed the environs of the boy's aching tooth. When this failed to relieve the boy of his pain, Grandpa said with some vehemence: "There's got to be a witch back of this! It's my guess that Spittle woman is up to her tricks again."

The next afternoon when Grandpa awakened from a catnap, he was surprised to see emerge from the cornfield below the house a white deer with an ear of corn in its mouth. When Jim came in from work and was told about the deer, he went out to see what damage had been done to his corn. He found the deer still there; it was going from row to row and jerking the ears of corn from the stalks and leaving them on the ground.

Jim hurried back to the house, got his rifle and returned to the cornfield. When he was within thirty feet of the deer he took careful aim and fired. The deer, however, showed no evidence of having been hit nor was alarmed at the noise of the gunfire; it continued to jerk corn from the stalks. Twice more Jim fired at the deer without any apparent effect on it. He could only shake his head in disbelief because he was sure he had not missed it.

When he learned what had happened, Grandpa shook his head, too. When he got excited, his short chin whiskers seemed to dance.

"That deer is bewitched!" he cried. "The Bible says, 'Thou shalt not suffer a witch to live.' "

When Grandpa suggested that a silver bullet be made from a dime with which to kill the deer and break the witch's spell, Jim thought of it as just another of his father's many superstitions. However, just to please him, he made a silver bullet and loaded his rifle with it.

Although night had come by this time, the moonlight was sufficient for Jim to see his way to the cornfield. When he located the deer, it stood facing him in a bold and defiant manner. Slowly and with great care he took aim and fired. The deer sprang into the air, then fell heavily to the ground. A trickle of blood oozed from the bullet wound above its left eye.

The most that had been expected from the use of a silver bullet was to break the hex power of Vergie Spittle; therefore, it was a distinct surprise to the Bonner family when word came that Vergie had been found dead in bed the next morning. The doctor who examined her reported that the cause of her death was a massive hemorrhage of the brain.

Murder in the Meadow

When Joe Harper and Vada Mounts were married on April 20, 1917, it came as a distinct surprise to the people of their community. Since Joe and Vada had never been more than casual friends and were never known to have gone out together on dates, people looked upon their marriage as somewhat unusual. It soon dawned on some of their acquaintances, however, that Joe might be looking for a way to avoid being drafted into military service. If that had been his motive, it failed to help him because, when his draft number came up, the selective service board ignored his marital status and instructed him to report to the induction center. Before leaving home, Joe warned the young men of the community to stay clear of his house and his wife while he was gone.

Before the year was out, Vada was notified that Joe was missing in action. Soon thereafter, Ramer Larch, a young man who lived on an adjoining farm, moved in with Vada. Even though there was outspoken disapproval of their living together under such an arrangement, they appeared to ignore the criticism completely. Ramer's friends reminded him of Joe's warning before he left home; moreover, they pointed out that it was possible that Joe was still alive and might return home without any forewarning. Ramer was not impressed with their admonitions and informed them that he would take his chances. Some people in the community hoped that the Red Men, a former local vigilante group,

21

would be revived to teach Ramer and Vada a durable lesson in proper behavior. If any action was ever taken toward a revival of that highly clandestine group, it came too late.

One afternoon when Ramer came in from work, Vada told him that she had seen a man standing at the timberline on the hill opposite the house. He was dressed in dark clothes and was accompanied by a black, shaggy dog. For several minutes he had stood there motionless while gazing intently down at the house, then abruptly had turned and disappeared into the woods. She led Ramer to the window to point out the place where she had seen the man; on looking up to the timberline they saw that he had returned and again was looking directly at the house.

Ramer and Vada then became extremely upset and for a time let their imaginations run wild. Among the ideas that raced through their minds were that the man might be Joe in disguise, or it could be some snooping neighbor, or perhaps it could be someone Joe had asked to check on his wife for him. As soon as the man had gone back into the woods, Ramer got his gun and, without saying a word about his intentions, slipped quietly out the back door.

Between the woods where the man had been seen and the top of the hill was a sloping meadow. When Ramer reached the top of that hill from the back side and looked down toward the meadow, he saw the man and the dog coming directly toward him. When the man was about half-way across the meadow, Ramer shot him down.

Unknown to Ramer, two boys who had been playing in the woods and had hidden in some bushes on hearing Ramer's approach, saw the shooting. They immediately ran home and reported it to their parents who, in turn, called the sheriff. By the time Ramer returned to Vada's house, the sheriff and a deputy were waiting for him there. With the two boys who had reported the incident leading the way, Ramer was taken by the sheriff and his deputy to the scene of the shooting.

They found the man lying face down in the meadow where he had fallen, with the big shaggy dog lying beside him. Their efforts to check the man closely, however, were thwarted by the vicious attitude of the dog. Not wanting to harm or destroy it, they decided to wait and try to find another way to retrieve the body. The sheriff and his deputy then took Ramer to the county jail to await further developments.

Three men of the community who had arrived at the scene proposed a plan by which the body could be safely removed. It was decided that one of the men would distract the dog's attention by getting it to chase him while the other two would rush in and carry the body away. One of the men, Deeter Amos, volunteered to lure the dog away. Although he realized it would be a most hazardous undertaking, it was either to do that or assist in getting the corpse; he could not bear the thought of touching a dead body. Many times after this event, Deeter related in his inimitable manner what transpired at that time.

"When I approached within twenty feet of the body," Deeter recounted, "that black, shaggy dog growled and bared his teeth in a vicious manner. To me, at that moment, he looked as big as a full-grown grizzly bear. When it got in a crouching position as if preparing to spring at me, I turned and started to run. I could hear it coming behind me as I ran at what I thought was my top speed. Then when I looked back and saw that dog nearly on me and its teeth flashing at my heels, I tell you I wasn't half running. Man, I took off like a bat out of Hades. When I came to a barbed wire fence, I sailed right over it and landed in a briar patch. By the time

I got out of there, I saw our plan had failed. That dog was then chasing the men toward the other end of the meadow and that dead man was still out there in the grass."

Since it was nearly dark by this time, it was decided that no further effort to recover the body would be made before morning. It was hoped that the dog, on learning that its master was dead, would voluntarily wander away.

Early the next morning when the men returned to the meadow, they could find neither the body of the man nor the dog. All subsequent searches of the surrounding area failed to locate them.

Also, that morning word came from the sheriff's office that Ramer was dead. It was clearly evident he had been choked to death. His neck was swollen and marks made about it by sharp fingernails were still clearly visible. Both the sheriff and the jailer emphatically stated that the jail had been locked all night and that it was impossible for anyone to have entered it without their knowledge.

Even though the coroner admitted it was practically impossible for a person to choke himself to death with his own hands, nevertheless he felt there was no other logical solution than to rule it as a suicide. Though there were some who thought otherwise, they sympathized with the coroner's position in that they realized how foolish it would make him appear in the eyes of the public were he to record that Ramer had been choked to death by a ghost.

The Prankish Triplets

In the vicinity of the boundary line which separates Clay and Roane Counties, there once lived a family with triplet sons. The three boys were so identical in appearance and mannerisms their own mother was often confused over their identities. The boys learned very early of their ability to confuse others and, whenever it could be used to their benefit, either as individuals or as a group, would take advantage of it.

In early boyhood the triplets became ill with measles and their mother became worried when they failed to "break out" as soon as expected. Since there was no doctor living in the community whom they could call in times of illness, the people had to try home remedies as the occasion might require. In this instance, after trying some of the more common remedies on the boys without success, the mother decided to brew up some "sheep tea", an odoriferous concoction that was not only unpalatable but highly offensive to persons of a squeamish nature.

As the mother approached the bed wherein the three boys lay, with a dose of the tea for the first one, they began to protest despite their wretched condition. She firmly seized the boy lying at the front side of the bed and poured a generous serving of the tea down his gagging throat.

While the mother returned to the kitchen to get the next dose of tea, the boy in the middle quickly climbed over his brother and forcibly took front position thus putting that already nauseated boy in line for the second dose. When the mother returned to the bedside, the protests made by the child now in the middle were ignored and he was promptly given another spoonful of the nasty tea.

As soon as the mother left the room to get the final dose, the third son, on seeing the successful maneuver of his brother, now climbed into the middle position and shoved his ill-starred brother to the backside of the bed. On the mother's return to the bedroom, she was still unaware of the switching of positions by the triplets and demanded of the one at the back to take his dose as a dutiful son should. At this point the other two sons responded to the aid of their mother by holding their brother while she gave him a third dose of the tea.

It was said that the measles truly "broke out" profusely on all three of the boys, but no evidence was established on whether the one who was given the triple dose of sheep tea had more measles than his brothers. It is true, however, much to the chagrin of the victim of the prank, the other two derived much enjoyment in later years whenever they told, far and wide, the tale of their boyish prank on their brother.

Centralia's Headless Ghost

At the time of the building of the West Virginia and Pittsburgh Railroad (now the B and O) from Buckhannon to Camden-on-Gauley around 1890, many people came here to work on the construction. Among those who came was Jacob Beamer, who became a legendary character in that area, especially among the young people who knew him.

Beamer was in his forties at the time and, as far as known, had never married. Before coming here he had attended an Eastern college but had dropped out before completing work for a degree. He had said there was a roving spirit within him which would not let him settle down at one place for any great length of time. When not working on the railroad, he would have an audience of young people who would be enthralled with his telling of highly imaginary tales. One story he told was about his ancestors' guardian moon ghost. As Beamer told it, his ancestors had originally come from the moon. His guardian ghost had explained to him how the Beamer family, while on a visit to the earth, had become stranded here -- and a lucky day it was for them.

A very long time ago the moon was much closer to the earth than it is now, Beamer related. It was a miniature earth with an atmosphere and inhabited by beings not unlike earth people. Then it took only a brief time to travel, by moonbeams, from luna firma to terra firma.

Then a terrible event occurred. A monstrous-sized meteor

came through the heavens so close to the earth that this planet was thrown off-balance, its land mass was broken into continents, and the earth's poles changed locations. This meteor struck the moon with such force it flattened the side which faces the earth, hooved out the back side, and made it a lop-sided planet. Moreover, the moon was forced out into space thousands of miles and its rotating mechanism was destroyed. As the meteor passed across the face of the moon, it cut a huge gash a mile wide and hundreds of feet deep and then sped on into outer space.

The stopping of the moon in its rotation brought alternating periods of burning and freezing which destroyed all life there and made it a place of desolation. The Beamer family, with no home to go back to, made adjustments quickly to living on earth, thanks to their guardian moon ghost who came here to watch over them. Free of the embellishments that normally characterized Beamer's discourses, that was the gist of his story of his family's origins.

It was well known among those who were acquainted with Beamer that he liked to take long walks alone at night, especially in the moonlight. Some believed he did this so that he could privately commune with his moon ghost. It was while he was on one of those nocturnal strolls that he was run over by a train as it passed through a deep cut in the hill near the village of Centralia, which is located some thirteen miles up the Elk Valley above Sutton. Because the accident happened at night, no one was aware of it until the next day when he was found lying beside the track. The body was headless; even though many people searched the environs for the missing head, it was never found.

The local legend is that when the moonbeams shine down the mountainside into the deep cut on a certain night of the year and at the exact time of the accident which took Beamer's life, a gray ghost leads a headless man, presumably Beamer, through the pass. Their movement is slow, the ghost looking along each side of the tracks apparently in search of Beamer's head. On reaching the far end of the cut, they follow the moonbeams up the mountainside and pass out of sight.

The last time Beamer and his ghost were seen, it is believed, was during the Great Depression. A deer hunter from Pittsburgh had set up his tent near the deep cut. On the second night he was there, he saw the ghost lead Beamer through the pass in the same slow, searching manner he had done when observed before. However, this time they did not go up the mountainside but suddenly disappeared on the other side of the pass.

While wondering what might have happened to them, the hunter chanced to look to the rear. Standing there, less than thirty feet away, were the headless Beamer and his ghost plainly silhouetted against a dense cluster of bushes. With his right hand, Beamer clutched a hand of the ghost while in the crook of his left arm he held what appeared to be a white skull. After looking directly at the hunter for a spine-chilling moment, the ghost led Beamer into the bushes and disappeared from view.

Ramp Power

Uncle Lige Morris was well-known for his high regard for the truth. Always judicious and circumspect in his speaking, he maintained a reputation throughout a long lifetime for reasonableness of thought and credibility -- with one exception that defied his sincerity and made him uncomfortable to think about as long as he lived. The story he brought back from a trip through the ramp country in the central Alleghenies was so out of character for him to relate that his friends wanted some time to think about it before accepting it as fact -- an act which Uncle Lige never forgot nor forgave.

It was in early April in 1905, while in the prime of life, that Lige mounted his best saddle horse and rode across the Alleghenies to visit relatives in Greenbrier County. The trip over was uneventful; however, on his return, in an effort to follow a short cut, he became confused and for some time wandered futilely through dense woodlands. Darkness came and, because of the danger of being struck by low-hanging tree limbs, he had to dismount and lead his horse. The trail soon became so steep and uneven he felt it to be too hazardous to walk in front of his horse so he gave his steed free rein while he walked behind and held onto its tail. At length they came out in a clearing on the mountainside where a large two-story log house loomed up a short distance ahead. It was here in this house that Lige found lodging for the night -- a night which he wished many times later, for peace of mind, he had never known.

As Lige lay in a comfortable bed in a room adjoining the living room, he could only reflect in amazement at the rapidity of the events that had transpired since his arrival here. In only a few minutes' time, his horse had been stabled and fed, he himself had been given food and drink and then had been peremptorily ordered to bed. Throughout this time, other than revealing that his name was Sol Jenkins, his host had been practically uncommunicative. He could now hear him puttering about in the kitchen and occasionally muttering to himself. Despite his peculiar situation, Lige, bone-tired and weary from his trip, soon drifted off to sleep.

Sometime later in the night he awoke to the pungent odor of cooked ramps which nearly overwhelmed him. His bedroom door was slightly ajar and on looking out, he saw two wizened old men with bushy white hair and unusually long beards sitting before the fireplace and engaged in an animated conversation. They talked in hoarse whispers often punctuated with high-pitched whistling noises. On a table between them were two stoneware mugs from which they occasionally took long draughts with gusto.

After a time, their conversation gradually subsided and then all was quiet again. The old men had fallen asleep in their chairs. Then Lige saw his host come in and pick up the men, one under each arm, and with their long beards dragging on the floor, carry them upstairs.

The next morning when Lige arose, he found his breakfast already prepared. He noticed, too, that his horse was saddled and ready for him at the front gate. So, with haste he made his departure and felt a great sense of relief once he was on his way again.

About two miles down the mountainside, Lige came to

31

another house where a man was in the wood-lot cutting firewood. Here he learned more about the old men. The woodcutter informed him that Sol Jenkins was the son of one of the aged men and the grandson of the other. The two old men slept upstairs, remaining in a coma until the arrival of mid-April each year. Shortly after the stroke of midnight on April 15, they aroused themselves from their long sleep, came down to their chairs before the living room fireplace and, while drinking ramp juice, talked about their experiences of earlier years. The older one often spoke of the time he spent as a Virginia militiaman at the Battle of Point Pleasant in 1774, while the other liked to tell of his exploits while serving under the command of Mad Anthony Wayne. On the basis of these claims, the older one was at least 150 years old and his son was close to 130. Lige could only stare in disbelief when he was told that Sol, who appeared to be in his early sixties, was actually approaching the age of 100. Moreover, it could be expected that he, too, would soon join his father and grandfather in the long sleep.

"Why do they sleep so much and live so long?" Lige asked.

"Some people say it's the ramp juice," the woodcutter replied. "They tell me those old men are so saturated in ramp juice they can't stay awake and so well-preserved they can't die. But I say there's more to it than ramp juice. I think they've sold their souls to the Devil. And who'll take care of them when Sol joins them in the long sleep? Well, I'm not waiting around to see. As soon as the roads are fit, I'm moving my family off this mountain. I tell you, there's something diabolical going on up there."

When Lige returned home and related this experience to his friends, its reception was so poor he never mentioned it again. But each year when springtime came and people began to talk about and prepare for ramp dinners, that far-away look would come into his eyes and everyone knew he was wondering about the fate of the three old men in the mountains.

Deloris the Slave Girl

A traveler on the highways and byways of Appalachia will occasionally come upon a hamlet whose name may stimulate his imagination much beyond what he actually sees. Few will there be, however, who would permit themselves to speculate to the extent of the bizarre events which occurred at Burnt House, a village located sixteen miles to the west of Glenville.

When the Staunton to Parkersburg Turnpike was being built through Western Virginia, many people were attracted to it as a passageway to the West and, for some, as a location of new business establishments. Among these was Jack Harris of New York, who while on the way West with his son, William, and three slaves, decided to build a tavern at the present site of Burnt House.

The tavern was a two-story log structure with a glass-windowed lookout, a practical addition often found on frontier structures. In time, the Harris Tavern became a regular stagecoach stop for passenger and mail service as well as headquarters for pack peddlers.

When Deloris, a beautiful Negro slave at the tavern, appeared in new dresses and adornments commonly sold by peddlers, local gossips took notice and began to speculate over the source of her good fortune. It was commonly known that Deloris and William Harris were quite fond of each other. Soon it was noticed that some peddlers who arrived here laden with heavy packs of goods disappeared overnight. A most damaging rumor was related by a Harris Tavern stable boy who told of seeing William Harris, with one swipe of a razor-sharp corn-cutting knife, cut off the head of a pack peddler. The body of the peddler was then dragged by William, with the help of a slave, across the turnpike and up a ravine now known as Dead Man's Hollow. Meanwhile, Deloris disposed of the head and cleaned up the gory mess.

These rumors spread far along the course of the turnpike and westward travelers were warned not to stop over night at the Harris Tavern. The business of the stagecoach company was so affected that it secured the services of the Pinkerton Detective Agency to investigate. Immediately Jack and William Harris sold the tavern, along with Deloris and another slave, to the widow Susan Groves and went west under the aliases of Jeff and Tex Howard.

One Sunday morning when Parson Woodford was going into the third hour of his "fire and brimstone" sermon, some members of the congregation became restless when the odor of something burning came to them. An inquisitive young man opened the church door and promptly announced that the tavern was afire. As the people approached the burning building, they saw a person swaying and dancing in the glass-enclosed lookout. It was Deloris, the slave girl, in her finest raiment, dancing and singing while the building burned. The fire was out of control, making it impossible to rescue her. While the people watched, the lookout, with Deloris inside, fell through the second-story ceiling and disappeared from view. Deloris had been extremely unhappy in her new situation and this act of self-immolation was her chosen way of escape.

After the tavern burned, stagecoaches continued to stop

at the hitching post in front of the "burnt house" to deliver the mail. Thus it was that the village of Burnt House got its name.

As local legend has it, Deloris, in spirit, returned to the community a number of times after her tragic demise. Usually on damp, foggy nights she came, at first a wavering flame, then taking the form of a young girl, she would dance over the ruins of the old tavern and finally drift over Dead Man's Hollow with a plaintive moan.

On a certain day in 1882, about thirty years after the tavern burned, this phenomenon of Deloris' reappearance occurred for the last time. It is of interest to note here that on that same day, fate caught up with William Harris, alias Tex Howard, when he was hanged in Texas for robbery and murder. In the community of Burnt House a terrifying electrical storm swept across the valley. Daylight turned to near darkness. Torrential rain and gusty winds bent huge trees to the ground while thunder shook the earth and balls of fire rolled down the turnpike.

In the midst of the tempest Deloris came and, after dancing for a brief time over the old tavern site, she drifted off toward Dead Man's Hollow where her last agonizing wail mingled with the storm. Today the traveler will find that the tranquil environment of the community of Burnt House belies its historic and legendary past.

A Suppressed Confession

On a flat upland area near the head of Naked Creek was the home of John Perry Bailes. The mention of his name often brought a hush to any conversation among adults and anxiety and fear to the youth who had heard about him. At the fireside on long winter nights, parents related to their children the story how John Perry and two other men had murdered old Ben Lough, but for lack of evidence had never been brought to trial. After the murder, John Perry's alleged accomplices had gone elsewhere to live, but John Perry had remained at the old family homestead where he and his wife, Elvira, kept much to themselves. It was said that shortly before the two men left the community, they met with John Perry in a secret rendezvous where the three took an oath that if any one of them ever confessed to the crime, or implicated the others, it would be the sworn duty of the other two to kill him.

Because of John Perry's crippled condition -- his left leg had been severed at the knee in a sawmill accident some years before -- he did little farming but made his living largely by buying and selling cattle. This usually meant long trips on horseback for him because the people of his community refused to deal with him. Many times the people who lived along Naked Creek saw John Perry return from a buying trip, riding ahead of a herd of young calves with strange men as drovers walking behind them. He sat astride his horse in a peculiar manner with his body leaning far forward, the foot of his good leg in a stirrup while his wooden pegleg pointed to the front in a dipping, wagging motion. From his back pocket protruded a large black billfold which was attached to a gold chain that extended from his belt. The wide brim of his soft black hat waggled with the jog of his horse and in unison with the bobbing of his wooden leg.

One night when John Perry was riding up the road about three miles below his house, the ghost of old man Lough came out from the bushes and leaped astride behind him. He tried to elude the ghost by making his horse gallup at full speed. On and on they raced through the night until the horse's sides were covered with sweat and lather and bloody froth dripped from its mouth, but the ghost still sat behind him. On arriving at his front gate, John Perry leaped to the ground, hobbled inside the house and hurriedly locked the door.

"Mercy me, John Perry," Elvira exclaimed. "You look as if you'd seen a ghost!"

John Perry covered his face with his hands as he leaned against the wall and moaned, "I did, Virey, I did!"

Soon everybody in the whole community was talking about how the ghost of old Ben Lough was chasing John Perry Bailes. Time after time it rode home with him which so unnerved him he felt he could bear it alone no longer. In the midst of a revival meeting then being held at the Pine Grove Church, John Perry came in and, much to everyone's surprise, limped up the aisle to the mourners' bench. While the congregation sat in stunned silence, he nervously wrung his hands and jabbered incoherently. Then abruptly he turned and hobbled down the aisle toward the door, his wooden leg striking the bare wood floor with a noise that echoed throughout the sepulchral stillness of the church.

Soon from the woods at the side of the church came the voice of a man praying. The mournful voice grew louder and louder and became so doleful it brought a hush over the congregation. From the pulpit the minister intoned: "The way of transgressors is hard." Then looking toward the woods from which the praying voice came, he said: "I say unto you, John Perry Bailes, there is no forgiveness without repentence, and there is no repentence without full confession." From the congregation came a chorus of Amens.

John Perry did not return to the church and was never seen again by most of the people of the community; nor did they hear anything about him for several weeks. Then it was reported that he was seriously ill with a fever -- a fever so high his breath was said to have scorched the varnish on the head-board of his bed.

What little information the people got about his condition came mostly through Elvira's sister, Amanda. She was known throughout the community for her brusque, outspoken manner, no matter what the situation might be. On one of her visits to her brother-in-law's home, she peered down at him and matter-of-factly stated: "John Perry, it 'pears to me you're pert nigh the end of your bean row. From what I've heerd about you and from what I see now, I'd say it's time for you to 'fess up. If you don't, jest as sure as God made little green apples, he'll march you straight through the gates of hell when you die."

When John Perry became worse, it was reported that he had asked for a minister to come to his bedside, presumably to hear a deathbed confession. Suddenly his two former associates appeared and stated that they had come to help take care of John Perry during his illness and thus relieve Elvira of the whole burden of caring for him. From that point on, no one was permitted to enter his room, not even

Elvira nor the minister when he came.

Through the long gray afternoon and evening of that chilly November day and far into the night, no sounds came from John Perry's bedroom. Just as the clock on the mantelpiece was striking the hour of three in the morning, the bedroom door opened; then the two men appeared and solemnly announced that he was dead.

Immediately after John Perry's funeral, the two men again left the community never to return. It was generally believed by the people of the community that John Perry had wanted to confess his part in the murder of Ben Lough but his partners in the crime had suppressed it.

The Ghost
of the Confederate Soldier

When the Virginia Assembly, in April 1861, voted for an ordinance of secession from the Union, the counties in the Allegheny Highland of Western Virginia refused to go along. Subsequently, the Assembly passed a law to authorize the governor to organize ten or more guerrilla units, composed of refugees from the Allegheny section, and send them back to drive out the federal forces in an effort to recover the area for Virginia. Quite bitter over the fate of Western Virginia and fearful for the exposed Shenandoah Valley, Governor John Letcher enthusiastically organized the guerrillas who were euphemistically designated as rangers.

Governor Letcher also issued commissions to agents and sent them behind the Union lines for the purpose of recruiting their companies. It soon developed, however, that pro-Southern civilians as well as Confederate commanders in Western Virginia began to complain. Most of the new rangers, they rightly pointed out, were actually robbers who plundered Unionists, Confederates and neutrals with complete impartiality. They banded together in close-knit groups, sometimes living in caves or fortifying themselves in the mountains and made raids upon settlements throughout the area. One such group, the self-styled "Dixie Boys", specialized in stealing livestock wherever it might be found and were so successful the band became infamous throughout northwestern Virginia.

41

The Welch Glades near Cowen in Webster County served as a rendezvous for marauding guerrillas in the area of what is now central West Virginia. On one occasion they invaded and burned the town of Sutton. Federal troops, then stationed at Summersville, pursued these irregulars and killed six of them in the chase. Shortly thereafter, a large expedition of federal troops ended the depredations of this gang by an attack upon its base in the Glades, during which twenty-two members of the gang were killed and twenty-six houses burned.

Under conditions such as these, it was extremely hazardous for soldiers of either the Union or the Confederacy to return home on furlough. The annals of Western Virginia of that time reveal that many young soldiers were murdered at or near their homes while on leave by bushwhackers operating sometimes under the guise of legitimate troops.

One such incident involved a young Confederate soldier who returned on leave to visit his parents in Clay County. Because of the probable presence of pro-Union sympathizers and bushwhackers in the community, he waited until darkness came before he entered the valley where his parents lived. On arriving at his home, he quietly slipped into the house through the back door.

On the second night of his leave, the soldier walked over the hill through the woods to visit with his girl friend. His trip there and back was uneventful and it appeared there were no enemy soldiers or bushwhackers in the community at the time.

Now somewhat more emboldened, the soldier, on the night before he was to return to his camp, got on his father's horse and started out on the country road toward his girl friend's house. When he reached the crossroads about a half-mile from his home, he was bushwhacked, allegedly by two Union soldiers. They cut his throat, then tied him on his horse and started them back toward home. By the time the horse arrived back at the home stable, the soldier had bled to death. He was buried in a cemetery beside the road near the scene of the ambush.

In later years, some people who have been in the vicinity of the crossroads between 9:30 and 12:00 midnight have reported seeing the ghost of the soldier riding hurriedly along the road. He sat uneasily on his horse, with his feet out of the stirrups, and looked back often as if he expected someone to be in pursuit of him. Some observers have waited long after the ghost rode out of sight to see if anyone was following it but as far as known, no pursuer has ever been seen.

What Hath Been Wrought?

The people of Southern Appalachia are proud of their heritage of freedom. This is particularly so in the choice of their manner of worship. Many of those early immigrants to this new country came here because they were dissenters from established churches in their homeland. This belief in religious freedom today finds expression in a great variety of exercises among which are hundreds of churches that still follow many of the practices of the camp meetings of the early nineteenth century. In these churches, highly emotional services which are seldom less than four hours long and oftentimes extend to six hours or more are characterized by the singing of hymns, ecstatic dancing, hand-clapping, extemporaneous sermons by lay members, testifying, foot-washing, faith-healing, and speaking in tongues. In a few churches, some unorthodox additions, the origins of which date back only to the first quarter of this century, are snake-handling and the drinking of poison.

Some of the better known churches in West Virginia which permit their members the option of handling snakes and sipping strychnine are those at Scrabble Creek, Frazier's Bottom, Jolo, Meade, Rum Creek, and Camp Creek. These churches also permit the practice of the Kiss of Charity, or Holy Kiss. From a number of sources, a leading one being Robert K. Holliday's TESTS OF FAITH, the following composite account of the services at one of these churches is recounted.

One warm Saturday evening a larger than usual number of people had gathered at the Scrabble Creek Church of All Nations in Scrabble Creek Hollow near Gauley Bridge. Some had traveled many miles to participate in the services while others had come through curiosity because it had been announced that snake-handling would be a part of the worship service. Among the latter were Silas Harper and his wife.

Some months earlier, when Mrs. Harper suggested that they go to Virginia to observe a snake-handling service she had read about in a newspaper, her husband had replied: "I'm not yet sure I am ready for it. I'd rather it would come to me." Then on learning that there would be rattlesnakes at the Scrabble Creek Church near their home, Mr. Harper said: "Now, let's go up and see this." And on this evening he and his wife were seated in this crowded little church where they were about to witness some amazing incidents.

For a number of hours the service consisted of the singing of hymns, impromptu speeches of lamentation, self-criticism, and great joy. Shouts of "Amen" and handclapping often punctuated these exercises. Practically all of the proceedings were marked with high emotion and spontaneity.

Standing in the midst of the participants was a young woman from Fairmont whose white uniform-style dress seemed to set her apart from the others. The regular members of this church knew of her strange powers, and to them her appearance was one of radiance and purity. As she stood there clapping her hands in rhythm with the singing, over her visage came the shadow of deep grief. Those who knew her realized that she was experiencing in her mind, as she had done before, the imagined pain of the Crucifixion. So intense was her psychic image of the agony of the Cross that blood appeared on her head, on her hands, on her side, and on her feet. From the unbroken skin of her hands, a thin trickle of blood ran down each of her forearms and dripped from her elbows to the floor. The impact of her experience upon the congregation was profound. Some found it difficult to believe what they were seeing, while most became quiet and watched in awe.

The overseer of the church appeared behind the pulpit and in a loud voice quoted from the Book of Mark: "They shall take up serpents; and if they drink any deadly thing, it shall not hurt them; they shall lay hands on the sick, and they shall recover." From a glass half-filled with strychnine, he took a sip, and then said: "Bring out the serpents."

From a corner of the church, a wooden box was brought to the platform. The overseer, after giving the sides of the box a number of vigorous kicks, removed the lid and lifted out a squirming rattlesnake. Other members likewise picked up snakes and passed them around. An elderly man was bitten on the hand. After putting the snake back in the box, he calmly walked over to the kerosene lamp on the wall and held his hand over the open flame, all the while with a smile on his face.

A person leaned across the aisle and said to Mr. Harper: "That woman is going to bring a rattler and put it on you." Harper said to himself: "Oh, Lord, what will I do now?" As the woman approached with the snake, he thought: "Well, Lord, I was here first and I'm not running." In telling of this incident later, he said: "When I came to myself, that big rattler had his head up on my left ear, and I don't know if they put him on my lap or not, I suppose I was scared so bad."

Later in the snake-handling ritual, which lasted about twenty minutes, a snake thrust its fangs into a young man's face. Surprised and bewildered, he released his hold on it as he sank to the floor on his knees. Immediately relatives and friends gathered about him and began to pray for his recovery.

Then someone shouted: "The snake's loose! The rattler's loose!"

There was a sudden outward dispersion of the less brave of the crowd through the door and windows. What had been a test of faith for some now became a test of speed for others. The commotion quickly subsided when all the snakes were returned to the box. The young man on the floor, now in a state of delirium, was picked up by two men and carried out of the church. Gradually the praying and chanting ceased and the service came to an end.

After the people had departed, the valley again became quiet and serene, the stillness only occasionally broken by a whippoorwill's call from far up on the mountainside. As they walked toward home in the dim light of approaching dawn, Harper, speaking to himself as much as to his wife, said: "As sure as every mountain has two valleys, I'm just as sure of myself now. I've found a power greater than my fear of serpents. I'll be going back."

A Hog Cried in Upshur

One spring day several years ago a migrant band of gypsies set up temporary housekeeping in and around an old abandoned farmhouse in Upshur County. While the gypsy men were traveling about the surrounding countryside trading horses, their womenfolk visited nearby homes and offered to tell fortunes. Often while the fortune-telling was in progress in the living room of a country home, gypsy children surreptitiously appeared in other rooms about the house and, if not detected and restrained, would carry off anything that struck their fancy. This petty thievery soon brought a wave of resentment against the gypsies and in a short time the people of the community closed their doors to all of them. Whether it was the cold attitude of the community toward the gypsies or their natural urge to move on that started them moving again is not known. Nevertheless, it was a pleasant surprise for the people when they learned that the gypsies, early one morning, had rounded up all their horses and ponies and moved out. Thereafter the old house where they had lived became known as the "Gypsy House."

One night while Hudson Thompson was passing the old Gypsy House, he heard a hog grunting -- a sound similar to that made by a distressed sow at the time her piglets are taken away from her. Even though the sound was distinct and apparently close behind him, he could not see the source of the sound. Hudson did not feel afraid but decided to walk a little faster anyway. His rapid walk soon became a jog and before he realized it he was running at full speed. It mattered not how fast he ran, he was unable to escape from the plaintive cry of the invisible hog. It was not until he had entered his own yard and closed the gate that the hog ceased its cry.

When two of the Fisher brothers went out to look for groundhogs one evening, they were surprised to see their dogs, bristling and whimpering, come rushing back to them. Then the boys heard the grunting and squealing of the phantom hog as it came closer and closer. One of the boys fired his gun in the direction from which the sound came, but the grunting continued unabated. Thoroughly shaken, the boys and their dogs all scrambled for home.

On another occasion a group of children of the community went out to pick blackberries on the abandoned farm back of the Gypsy House. Soon after arriving there, they heard the cry of the phantom hog. As it came closer, their dog began to growl and back away from something they could not see. The children fled in all directions; some climbed up in nearby trees while others perched themselves atop a rail fence. For several minutes the dog ran in circles and barked at the crying hog no one could see. Then they heard the sound go toward the Gypsy House and the dog made no effort to follow it.

Since practically all those who had heard the phantom hog and reported it were young people, most of the adults of the community were reluctant to admit any credence in the reports about it. Two men who thought there might be some truth to what the children had reported but did not want to admit it for fear of being laughed at, decided to go out and see for themselves. By the ruse of going hunting for some raccoons that had been playing havoc in their corn-field, they really intended to put an end to the phantom hog.

There was a full moon shining brightly as the men went out into the night with their rifles and a 'coon dog on a leash. As they approached the old Gypsy House, they heard the phantom hog grunting in the bushes back of the house. This time it did not come out as it had done on previous occasions but remained in the bushes and cried continuously. The men crept closer to the bushes with their rifles at the ready while the dog, still leashed, bristled and growled as it followed at their heels.

When they came up to the clump of bushes, one of the men, with his rifle barrel, carefully lifted a limb aside in order to see underneath the bushes.

"Oh, my heavens, just look there!" he exclaimed.

Sticking out from beneath a pile of dried and broken twigs was a tiny baby's hand. The men quickly removed the twigs and found the corpse of a very young child. Strangely enough, the sound of the crying hog ended the moment they found the infant's body. The following day, the baby was properly buried in a local cemetery and the cry of the hog was never heard again.

Solly's Christmas Tree

When the first settlers migrated into the Allegheny Mountains in pre-Revolutionary times, they found the area a wild and rugged region of lofty mountain ranges separated by narrow valleys and over all a dense primeval forest. Within its depths were such lurking dangers as the panther, the black bear, and an occasional band of Indians on the trail of game or revenge. Because of the dangers they faced, the settlers usually located their first home at a ledge against the mountainside. From this practice came a widespread frontier saying. When people wanted to wish happiness and a more secure way of life for another, they would say: "May the sun shine in your back door some day."

Such was the time when the parents of Solomon Carpenter came over the mountains from eastern Virginia and made their first home on a ledge of a mountainside near the place where Camp Run enters into the Elk River. Later, a lean-to addition was made to their ledge home and it was here that Solomon, or Solly, as they called him, was born.

As family legend has it, when Solly was five or six years old, a Christmas tree was prepared for him which, perhaps, was the first Christmas tree rite observed in Western Virginia and to which this family owed its survival. A tall holly tree nearby their home was chosen for the event and at its top a rosin-covered cross was tied with deerskin thongs. When the night of Christmas came, the cross was set afire.

51

Unknown to the Carpenter family, a band of Indians was hiding in the woods below the ledge home. These Indians, shortly before this, had killed all the members of another family only a short distance from here, and now they were waiting to attack the Carpenter family when darkness came.

After blazing brightly for some moments, the cross burned free from its mooring and plunged down the hillside into the area where the Indians were hiding. The Indians, who had some knowledge of the Christian religion and its emblem of the cross, saw this as an act toward them of a vengeful God and fled in fear and confusion.

Several years later one of these Indians returned to the area on a scouting expedition and after killing a deer, was attacked by a panther and mortally wounded. Solly Carpenter, by then a teenager, found the Indian and from whom learned, before he died, how that Christmas tree in Solly's youth had saved the lives of his family.

Tragedy in Booger Hole

In Otter District of Clay County, some forty miles south of Glenville as a sober crow flies, is a place called Booger Hole. The events which so firmly stamped upon the area the name it bears have become the source of traditional narrations from older to newer generations while families gather at their fireplaces on long winter evenings.

The area of Booger Hole, just prior to World War 1, was occupied by about a dozen families of questionable repute. A local chronicler wrote that they "farmed a little during the day, drank hard liquor in the evening, loved hard at night, and fought hard among themselves in their spare time." Much to the dismay of their neighbors, they often frolicked and danced to the weird strains of mountain music from sunset to dawn. Their obnoxious reputation became common knowledge throughout the county and no one who valued his life would dare go there, especially after dark. In order to discourage the children from being drawn, through curiosity or otherwise, into the area, parents began to call it Booger Hole.

Late one evening, Henry Harless, an unsuspecting pack peddler, wandered into the area and was never seen again. An aged woman resident, who claimed to possess the power of witchcraft, boasted that she could light her corncob pipe and before it burned out, could lay her hand on the grave of the peddler. Soon after this, as she sat in a rocking chair near an open window in her home, an unknown person shot her. No one was ever apprehended for these murders.

Preston Tanner's father owned some rich farm land which extended into Booger Hole. Following Preston's marriage, this land was ceded to him and his wife, Ellen. Against the advice of friends, they built a house there and made it their home.

Soon after the arrival of the newlywed couple into the community, a young man there by the name of Howard Sampson was struck by the beauty of Ellen Tanner. He spoke of her as being "purty as a red bird" and that he intended to take her away from her husband, even if he had to kill him and burn his victim's house down.

A few weeks later, Sampson found the opportunity to stay overnight at the Tanner home while Ellen was spending the night with her parents. During the night, as Sampson related later, when he awakened, most of the house was engulfed in smoke and flames and he was barely able to escape alive. Preston Tanner was not so lucky; his body was recovered later from the smouldering ruins. When a subsequent inspection indicated that Tanner had met with foul play before the house burned, young Sampson and his father were arrested and taken to the Clay County jail. The elder Sampson was accused of being an accessory to the crime.

News of the event spread like wildfire and feelings ran high against the Sampsons. Good men temporarily lost their reason when they joined in mob action for the purpose of lynching the accused men. Disguised in sheets and pillow cases, they roamed the streets of the town in search of the deputy sheriff who had the key to the jail. After failing to find the deputy, who spent the night hiding in the attic of a neighbor's house, the mob was convinced through the eloquence of attorney Davenport that the law should be permitted to take its course. When daylight came, Sheriff Stephenson had the prisoners removed to Webster Springs for safekeeping until the time of the trial.

The trial of the Sampsons, father and son, ran for several days and was a major attraction in that area at the time. In the presentation of the state's case, the prosecuting attorney directed the chief prosecution against the son. On one occasion, he gave the spectators in the courtroom a pleasant shock when he departed from his usually calm and discreet manner to speak of the defendant as "an illiterate, weasel-eyed moron." The trial ended with the elder Sampson being released and the son sentenced to prison for life.

A short time later, an order went out to all the people of Booger Hole to move elsewhere and never return. After their departure, all the houses of the area were burned to the ground. In spite of this act on the part of the citizenry to cleanse the place with fire, Booger Hole remains a figurative blight on the countryside.

The Ghost of Zona Shue

In the annals of Greenbrier County can be found the unique fact of the admission to court record of the testimony of a ghost. The events that led up to that bizarre experience occurred in a rural community east of Rainelle in 1897.

In a neat little cottage in that community, Mary Heaster, a middle-aged widow, lived alone. Hour after hour, late into the night she lay awake and reviewed in her mind all the things she could remember having heard or observed about her son-in-law, Edward "Trout" Shue. She recalled the time when this brawny, ruggedly handsome young blacksmith and stone-mason first came to the community and how excited the young ladies were about his arrival. Then there was the surprising news that one of his admirers, Esteline Cutlip, had run away from home to marry him. After their marriage, they had returned to the community and started housekeeping in a log cabin across from the Rock Camp Church.

Sometime after their baby girl was born, it was observed that Trout rarely did any work and neglected to provide for his family. Ominously one dark winter night three men appeared at the front door of his cabin and told him, in no uncertain terms, to go to work and get food and clothes for Esty and the baby. When Trout failed to do as ordered, the three men returned, over-powered him and dragged him to a creek nearby. After cutting a hole in the ice, they ducked him in the cold blue water.

One morning soon thereafter while making up the bed, Esty found a razor under Trout's pillow. Thoroughly alarmed, she wrapped up the baby and left home never to return.

After Trout had married again, it was rumored that he was so jealous of his second wife he forced her to go with him and help him in his work as a stone-mason. One day while helping him build a chimney, she would fill a container with rocks which he then pulled up by a rope to his work platform. Once as she bent over to fill the container, Trout dropped a rock on the back of her head, causing concussion and sudden death.

Then Mary Heaster's daughter, Zona, fell in love with Trout. Despite Mary's pleading and begging her not to marry him, she ignored her mother's disapproval and became his third wife.

Zona, at the time of her marriage, was a strong and healthy young woman who had never had a serious illness in her whole lifetime. Thus it was an astounding shock to the whole community when word came that she was dead. Dr. Knapp, the community doctor, on checking her death, reported that her heart had failed her.

Now that Zona was dead and buried, Mary could only lie sleepless, or at best toss in fitful slumber, at night and wonder what had really happened. She had some doubts about Dr. Knapp's report on the cause of her daughter's death and she fervently prayed that she might learn how Zona had really died.

In her fitful slumber Mary thought she heard noises about the house, but on becoming fully awake, all was quiet. Later in the night while she dozed, she was disturbed by hearing someone calling her. On awakening she saw a pale silhouette of Zona standing at the doorway of her bedroom. When Mary sat up in bed, the apparition disappeared. Just to make certain she was not dreaming, she arose and looked throughout the house and out the windows into the night, but all was quiet and serene.

A few night's later, Zona's ghost reappeared at Mary's bedroom door and pleaded, "Mother, Mother, please help me!" Mary, although thoroughly frightened, arose and followed the ghost to the back door. From there she watched it walk out through the apple orchard toward the Soul Chapel Cemetery where Zona had been buried.

The next appearance of Zona's ghost was frightfully disturbing to Mary. It was while she was on her knees praying that she felt a hand on her shoulder and on looking up she saw the ghost standing beside her. It related in great detail how Trout had murdered Zona: because she had prepared a meal without any meat, he had become so angry he clasped her head in his huge hands like a vice and with a sudden twist had broken her neck.

After the ghost had left, Mary remained sleepless throughout the remainder of the night. Her mind was wracked with worry over what she should do. The next day she went to her neighbors and told them all that had happened. After some discussion it was decided that the proper authorities should be notified. Mary, accompanied by some neighbors, went immediately to the county seat at Lewisburg and reported the happenings to the prosecuting attorney. Soon thereafter, steps were taken to hold an inquest.

Zona's body was exhumed and removed to the Nickel schoolhouse for the inquest and autopsy. In addition to Dr. Knapp, Dr. Rupert, a surgeon, and Dr. Machesney were appointed to perform the autopsy. A jury of six persons, led by constable Shawver, was brought to the schoolhouse to observe the proceedings. When Trout Shue asked if he might attend the inquest, the authorities refused to grant his request.

It was at the inquest that it became public knowledge for the first time that Trout had personally prepared his wife's body for burial. He had dressed her in a frilly, high-necked dress with a large bow below the chin. It was thus that she appeared when Dr. Knapp had checked; however, he admitted his examination had been somewhat hastily made because of the agonizing grief being expressed by Trout at the time over the loss of his wife.

After the body was removed from the coffin and placed on a table, Dr. Rupert examined the stomach to see if there was any poison present, but found none. At this point one of the jurors asked Dr. Rupert why the woman's head had seemed to roll loosely when the body was placed on the table. An examination was then made of the neck and it was found to be broken.

Following the inquest Trout was arrested and taken to the county jail in Lewisburg to await trial on the charge of having murdered his wife. Some people were so incensed over what Trout was accused of doing, they looked upon a trial as a waste of time. When John Seward appeared with a rope and suggested a hanging party, he soon had a mob moving in the direction of the county jail.

When the sheriff learned of the approach of the mob, he handcuffed Trout to deputy John Dwyer and sent them into a cornfield to hide. There in the drizzling rain and within hearing distance of the angry mob, they sat out the night. Meanwhile, the sheriff convinced the mob the court should decide the fate of Trout Shue. When daylight came, he was safely returned to jail.

In the ensuing trial the testimony of Mary Heaster, including the information provided her by Zona's ghost, had a convincing effect on the jury. Trout was convicted of murder and sentenced to the state penitentiary at Moundsville for life. It was while there that he died in 1905.

A Mystic Remembrance

A commonly known feature of the culture of Southern Appalachian people is a belief of the existence of witches and ghosts. Not so well known is the belief they have that some people have experienced an earlier existence. In seeking an explanation for this, they speculate that such persons have either been reincarnated, or perhaps, in some mysterious way, have inherited the knowledge of some unusual or traumatic experience of some remote ancestor. As proof, they refer to the fact that small children often remember previous lives and whose mystic association with imaginary playmates sometimes results in strange stories that frighten and disturb their parents. In most instances, as the children mature, they outgrow those memories. However, there is an interesting, if dubious, tale of one person who did not outgrow a mystic remembrance of his early childhood, much to his distress.

Although an only child, this man vividly recalled even after reaching middle age, an experience of having observed his two older brothers kill a man and then bury his body in a shallow grave under the victim's house. On the following night, he recalled, he had helped his brothers remove the body to a limestone cavern near the top of a hill. Some distance inside the cavern, they placed the corpse on a ledge that slanted upward at the outer edge where it could not be seen by anyone passing through the cavern.

This remembrance of his having been a participant in a

61

serious crime sometimes struck the man with such force he would break out in a cold sweat and become so weakened he would have to lie down until it wore off. For many years he bore his affliction in silent despair; then by an odd turn of fate, an event occurred which only confounded him further.

While this man's son was a student at the University of Virginia at Charlottesville, one of the field-trip projects for a geology course he had there was to explore some caverns in the Blue Ridge area. Since he was an amateur photographer he, on this trip, took pictures of some of the caverns they visited. Some weeks later when he went home for the holidays, he took the pictures with him to show to his parents.

When his father saw the picture of an entrance to one of the caverns, he broke down and told his family, for the first time, about the burden of his lifetime; then pointed out the remarkable likeness of the cavern of his mystic experience to that of one his son had explored. At last the family knew the cause of the man's strange fainting spells.

When the son returned to school, he went back to that particular cavern to investigate it further; not that he attached any credence to the story his father had related, but to prove to his father it was all in his imagination and, hopefully, relieve him of further worry about it. A short distance inside the cavern he found a ledge similar in appearance to the one his father had described. He flashed a light up over the ledge and there he saw a human skeleton completely fossilized with limestone deposit.

The local authorities were immediately notified of the discovery of the skeleton. When a subsequent investigation was made, it was estimated, from the accumulated limestone deposit that had dripped down on the skeleton from a break in the ceiling of the cavern, that it had been there at least two hundred years.

In Judge Lynch's Court

On Christmas Eve in 1875, Thomas Lee was waylaid and murdered while crossing the Campbell's Creek bridge at Malden. The next day Rufus Estep and John Dawson were arrested on the charge of committing the crime and were taken to the Kanawha County jail in Charleston. In and around Malden on that Christmas Day, the murder of Lee, who was a highly respected citizen of the community, was the chief topic of conversation. The more the people thought about the crime the angrier they became and before the day ended a mob was formed to attempt to lynch the accused men.

While the mob was on the way to Charleston, Philip W. Morgan, high sheriff of Kanawha County, with the aid of his deputies, removed the prisoners to the jail in Barboursville, then the seat of government of Cabell County. Two days later, as an added precaution, Estep and Dawson were taken to the Wood County jail at Parkersburg.

On the convening of the Kanawha County Circuit Court in Charleston approximately three weeks later, the men were returned to the jail in Charleston to await trial. One month, to the day, after the murder was committed, the prisoners were taken into court and arraigned upon the charge of murder. Their attorneys, R. H. Freer and Abram Burlew, immediately requested a change of venue because, they informed the Court, there existed such a high degree of resentment toward the accused men it would be impossible to obtain a fair trial for them in Kanawha County. The attorneys for the State, John E. Kenna and James H. Ferguson, strongly opposed the motion and insisted that the trial begin at once. In deference to the defense, Judge Joseph Smith stated that he would announce his decision on the following morning. The prisoners were then returned to the Kanawha County jail.

On that same day in Charleston, Thomas Hines, a journeyman tailor, walked into a shoe shop on Anderson Street and, without provocation, cut the throat of J. W. Dooley, a black shoemaker, who bled to death soon thereafter. Hines was immediately arrested and lodged in the local jail.

When the people in Malden learned that Estep and Dawson had been remanded to the jail in Charleston, word was quietly passed around that Judge Lynch was going to take over the trial of the two men at nine o'clock that night at the jail house. All would-be participants were warned to enter Charleston surreptitiously so as not to attract any undue attention of the town's residents to what was transpiring.

Promptly at nine o'clock grim-faced men came into Charleston from all directions and surrounded the jailhouse. While they were taking Estep and Dawson from their prison cells, some fifty black men appeared and took out Hines. All then marched to Malden with their captives.

When they reached the iron bridge at Campbell's Creek where Lee had been murdered, Estep and Dawson were promptly hanged at the very spot where they had committed the crime. At a place some three hundred yards above the bridge, Hines was hanged by his black captors to a limb of a honey locust tree. As the mob dispersed, the bodies of the three men were left swinging slowly in the bitter cold winter wind as a grim reminder that the verdict rendered by Judge Lynch's Court had been carried out.

Case of the Damp Damsel

One sultry afternoon in midsummer, Hugh Nelson received a telephone call at his office in Morgantown requesting him to be in Marlinton early the next morning to close a timber deal. Because, at that time, the mountain roads were in poor condition and there was a storm brewing, he decided to set out on the trip immediately.

By the time Hugh arrived in the high Alleghenies, darkness had come and he found himself in the midst of a torrential thunderstorm. The brilliant, pulsating flashes of lightning created an eerie world about him and the ponderous rumble of thunder jarred the mountain and reverberated in the valley below. From roadside cliffs, rushing rivulets occasionally spouted into the roadway and splattered against his car as he passed; and high winds, at times, brought pieces of tree limbs hurtling about him and impeding his progress. Nevertheless, he felt he had no choice but to keep going because, he surmised, there was no human habitation within miles where he might seek refuge.

On rounding a sharp turn in the road, Hugh was surprised to see a young woman standing some distance ahead and waving an arm as a signal for him to stop. By the light of the flashes of lightning, he saw that she was dressed in bridal attire and that her rain-soaked, raven-black hair clung in disarray about her head and shoulders. As he slowed to a stop beside her, he noticed that she appeared to be in a state of shock; her eyes were dark and piercing and her face had an unnatural pallor.

In an excited voice she told him that she had just come up from the valley where a flash flood had washed out the bridge and that her girl companion had drowned there. She warned him not to take the road into the valley but to go down the mountain by another way.

When Hugh asked if he could be of any help to her, she replied that since her home was located on the alternate road which he could take, she would appreciate it if she could ride that far with him. Hugh opened the car door and she entered and sat beside him. Noticing that she appeared to be chilling, he got his coat from the back seat and placed it about her shoulders, an act she did not appear to notice. Then, following her directions, they soon found themselves on a narrow, graveled road winding into the countryside.

Even though it continued to rain in a steady downpour, the worst of the storm had passed. Only occasional flashes of lightning and muffled rolls of thunder came from far over the mountains to the east. As they rode along in silence, Hugh was curious about his passenger, but seeing the nervous state she was in, he dared not question her. However, she did tell him that her name was Janet Grey and that her home was some five miles distant from where they had met.

After what had seemed an interminable drive on this narrow road, they arrived at Janet's house. She thanked him and then hurried up the flagstone walk to the house. Hugh watched her go up the steps to the colonnaded porch; without a glance backward, she opened the door and went inside. He then resumed his journey, by way of the detour, toward Marlinton.

It was not until some time later that he remembered he had left his coat with Janet. Since it was out of the question to go back after it at this time of the night, he decided he would get it on his return the next day.

While in Marlinton Hugh learned that a flash flood had washed out the bridge that Janet had spoken of and that a man had drowned at the crossing place when he failed to see that the bridge was gone. However, no one seemed to have heard that anyone else had drowned there that night. The more Hugh thought about it the more he felt obliged to stop at Janet's home on the way back to thank her for the warning she had given him. To stop to get his coat now seemed to be of minor importance.

On his return trip, Hugh followed the country roads as well as he could remember. Even though there were not many landmarks that stood out in his memory from the night before, he was confident that he was on the right road. When a large white house with a colonnaded front porch came into view, he felt quite sure that it was Janet's house.

Hugh went to the front door and knocked. Presently the door opened and a white-haired, elderly woman appeared. As he told her about his experience of the night before, she looked at him with incredulity.

"Oh, no, you surely are mistaken!" she said in a hushed voice. "It couldn't have been my Janet, because she passed away five years ago. You must have met someone else."

Then she related how her daughter had lost her life. Janet had wanted to be married in the church which the family had attended when they lived on the other side of the valley. On the evening before her wedding, while on the way to the church for the rehearsal, she and a friend, who was to have served as a bridesmaid, drove into the river and were drowned. Her body was recovered soon thereafter and buried in the family cemetery located on a knoll back of the house.

Noting Hugh's look of unbelief, Mrs. Grey said: "Come

67

I'll show you her grave."

As they walked around the house toward the cemetery, Mrs. Grey continued to speak of her daughter in a low, even voice. At the backyard gate she paused briefly and then said: "It was so near to her wedding day, we decided to bury her in her bridal gown." Since Hugh had made no reference to Janet's attire in his conversation with Mrs. Grey, her speaking of it now left him visibly shaken. Misinterpreting Hugh's reaction, she added: "Some people thought it was unusual for us to do that, but we were sure Janet would have wanted it that way."

As they approached Janet's grave, they both stopped suddenly and stared in amazement; there, draped over the headstone on her grave, was Hugh's coat.

The Horse with a Halo

Many years ago on Leatherwood Creek in Clay County there appeared a large white horse with a halo. Although the members of the family who saw it described the event in different ways, there was general agreement that a glowing halo of soft light was seen above the horse wherever it went.

One evening after supper the family had gathered on the front porch of their house and were engaged in the lively pleasure of genial conversation. Then abruptly all talking stopped and everyone looked toward the highway. At some four hundred yards' distance, they saw a white horse coming up the highway. It walked with a spirited gait, its long white mane flowed back in the gentle breeze, and above it floated a halo.

When the family saw the horse turn off from the highway and start up the lane toward their house, they all ran inside and locked the door. From the windows they watched to see what the horse would do. With liveliness it came prancing up the lane alongside the whitewashed board fence. On arriving at the yard gate, it stopped momentarily; then with a toss of its head and a loud snort, it reared up and leaped over the gate into the yard and came on toward the house.

By this time the members of the family were quite excited. Some were running from one window to another to get a better view of the horse while others were looking for places to hide. Then the horse leaped, with a loud clatter, onto the front porch. It now appeared to be monstrously large, its eyes shining like coals of fire and above it was the halo.

When the horse began to stomp the front door down, the family escaped by way of the back door and ran some distance up the hill back of the house. There they hid behind some trees and waited to see what it would do.

In a short time they saw the horse back out of the house into the front yard and start to float upward in the air. Up and up it went until it passed out of sight. But the halo remained against the sky a long while after the horse had disappeared. No one has ever been able to find a rational explanation of this strange event.

A Gift for Angela

At the time of the oil and gas boom in the Blue Creek section of Kanawha County, a flood of newcomers moved into the area. Among those who came were Clyde and Asbury Carpenter who were employed as roustabouts in the oil field. Soon after their arrival, the brothers became acquainted with Angela Carter, an attractive young woman of Falling Rock whose affections they sought with considerable rivalry. Although Angela was disturbed at times over the heated arguments they had over her, she was secretly pleased about it and tried to be equally friendly with both of them.

In time, however, Angela fell in love with Asbury; they announced their engagement and began to make plans for a June wedding. Then the coming of World War I interrupted their plans. Both Asbury and Clyde were called by the selective service board to report for physical examinations preliminary to induction.

A few days after their examinations, the brothers were notified that Clyde had failed to qualify but Asbury was accepted and had one month to prepare for induction. Asbury and Angela hurriedly rearranged their wedding plans so they could be married before his departure. After they were married, they lived with Angela's parents until the time for Asbury to report to the induction center.

It appeared that Clyde had accepted Angela's choice without any bitter feelings. On the day of Asbury's departure,

Clyde accompanied his brother and Angela to the depot to see him off and to wish him well. As Asbury entered the train, Clyde called out to him, "Don't you worry about Angel Face, Asbury, I'll take good care of her for you while you're gone."

For two or three months after Asbury left, Angela received letters from him quite often; however, on his transfer to Europe he wrote less frequently and, in time, stopped altogether. In the meantime Clyde and Angela developed a closer relationship.

One evening when Clyde went to see Angela, he told her that he had heard some people down at Elkview talking about a big battle occurring in France, that Asbury's battalion was involved and had been totally wiped out. When Angela questioned the failure of the War Department to notify her about it if it were true, Clyde explained that, in a case such as this, it could be months before all the necessary notifications were officially delivered.

Angela did not fail to observe Clyde's kindness in breaking the sad news to her and, as a concerned brother-in-law, his generous offer to be available for any needs she might have. From this moment a deeper affection grew between them and, in time, Clyde talked her into marrying him.

On Christmas Eve while Clyde was decorating the tree in the living room of their home and Angela was in the kitchen, she heard the front door open. Then she heard Clyde say, "Well, well, if it isn't Asbury."

Out of sight in the kitchen, Angela stood as if petrified. Next came Clyde's pleading voice, "No, no Asbury, please don't shoot!" Then there was a sharp pistol shot.

Angela quickly regained control of herself. On rushing into the living room, she got a glimpse of a man in a soldier's uniform going out the front door and closing it behind him. On the floor lay Clyde with a bullet hole in his forehead.

Before Angela had time to recover from this initial shock, there was a light knock on the door. With a trembling hand she opened it and there stood a boy with a letter in his hand.

"A telegram for Mrs. Angela Carpenter, Ma'am," the boy said.

Angela quickly opened the envelope and with eyes brimming with tears began to read: We regret to inform you that your husband, Asbury Carpenter, was killed in action on December 21, 1917 . . . .

Campus Ghost

It is common knowledge in the community of Glenville that there is a ghost on the campus of the local state college. As far as known, it has never been seen but has been heard on numerous occasions by certain students, faculty members, and building caretakers as it passed through Verona Mapel Hall and Clark Hall presumably on the way to the cemetery adjoining the campus. It seems to linger longest in Clark Hall where late-working journalism students and members of the MERCURY staff have reported hearing it. So far, it appears to be a kind and pleasant ghost, and the only criticism heard about it is that it seems to be unusually awkward and clumsy as it moves about.

Why the ghost is there has been the subject of some speculation. Some believe there may be some connection between the ghost's appearance and the unresolved murder of a local resident some years ago. In the fall of 1918, a lady by the name of Lou "Sis" Linn, who lived in a house where Verona Mapel Hall is now situated, was bludgeoned to death and her assailant was never apprehended. Therefore, some believe this is Miss Linn's ghost searching for the murderer in the corridors of the buildings on the upper campus. Some close observers of the situation have reported that early morning commuters across that area of the campus have noticed that the cemetery gate, for some unknown reason, is often found open at that time of the day.

Spooks and Ferrididdles

Glenbernie Lodge was the name given to the mountain re-treat that Glenn and Bernice Stafford personally built in their leisure time. It was situated in a secluded spot, yet was easily accessible and only a few miles distant from their home in Elkins. Here in their serene sylvan second home they spent many happy weekends and vacations together.

In the 1930's, Glenn and Bernice moved to Cleveland where he was employed in a munitions plant and thereafter it was only on rare occasions they found the opportunity to return for brief visits to Glenbernie Lodge. During their ab-sence, however, Bud Slagle, a young man of their acquaint-ance while residing in Elkins, looked after the lodge for them. Although somewhat handicapped by having a club-foot, Bud was industrious and thoroughly dependable. True, he never answered Glenn's letters of instructions about caring for the property, yet he always did what he was asked to do.

Early one spring, Glenn had informed Bud he wanted cer-tain repairs made at the lodge in preparation for a short vaca-tion he and Bernice planned to spend there in early autumn of that year. Because of the noise and congestion of urban living, they longed to escape to the solitude of the mountains and, hopefully, once again experience the gentle pleasure of tranquil living.

On arriving at Glenbernie Lodge in the early afternoon of a calm September day, they were surprised to find that Bud had not completed the work he had been asked to do; in fact it appeared he had only just begun. After unloading the car, Glenn decided to drive down to Elkins and try to locate Bud, leaving Bernice to unpack and store away their supplies.

Sometime later in the afternoon while Bernice was in the bedroom, she distinctly heard someone walking through the hallway outside her bedroom door. She recognized at once the scuffing sound of Bud's club-foot as it scraped the hardwood floor. She surmised that Glenn had found Bud and had brought him back to help make the repairs needed at the lodge. However, on opening the door and looking out, she saw no one. She then went outside and looked all about the lodge. The only living thing she noticed was a ferrididdle which scampered out from behind a tree and disappeared around a back corner of the lodge.

Glenn returned shortly thereafter with the information that Bud had gone to Cumberland to visit a sister back in April and no one remembered having seen him since. It appeared that if any repairs were to be made, Glenn would have to make them himself -- a thought that left him in a not-too-happy frame of mind. Therefore, it was with some reluctance that Bernice told him about the noise she had heard in the hallway. As she expected, he began to tease her about her "unbridled imagination."

Shortly after dark that same evening when Bernice went out on the front porch, she noticed some lights in the woods far down below the lodge. They appeared to be the headlights of a car moving slowly up the valley. She listened for the sound of a motor but could hear none. When she informed Glenn about it, he came outside and joined her. After watching the lights for a few moments, he said in a hushed voice: "Why, that can't be a car, Bernice; there's no road down there."

As they watched, they saw the lights rise above the tree-tops and move slowly toward them. At a point some three or four hundred yards distant, the lights stopped momentarily, then moved back into the valley. For a half-hour or so the lights continued to move back and forth and each time seemed to come a little closer to the lodge.

Throughout the whole time, Glenn and Bernice were fascinated by this phenomenon. However, when they saw the lights come up and disappear behind the lodge, they became somewhat alarmed. Glenn hurriedly got a flashlight and they both went out to investigate. Only a short distance behind the lodge they saw a dull light glowing from the trunk of a fallen tree.

"It's only foxfire!" Glenn exclaimed as he touched the glowing wood with his hand. "I don't know, but it's my guess those lights we saw must have been some sort of phosphorescent gas floating through the air."

As they were returning to the lodge, a ferrididdle cut across their path almost underfoot and rustled the leaves as it fled into the darkness. Bernice was startled by its sudden appearance and Glenn admitted he could not remember ever having seen one out at night before.

Soon after they had gone to bed that night, they heard someone walking through the hallway. It was the same scuffing sound Bernice had heard there in the afternoon. Suddenly both sat bolt upright. The footsteps had stopped just outside their bedroom door. Glenn felt for the handgun and flashlight on the nightstand, then quietly got out of bed and moved toward the door.

The footsteps were then heard again as they moved out the hall toward the living room. Quickly opening the door, Glenn flashed the light out into the hall, but he could see no one. At that moment Bernice gave a blood-curdling scream.

Glenn rushed back to her only to find that a ferrididdle had run across the bed and in its fright had leaped upon her head.

Bernice was thoroughly unnerved and sat on the side of the bed sobbing softly. Although Glenn was a little shaken himself, he sat down beside his wife and put his arm about her shoulders. His efforts to console her eased her fright after some time; nevertheless, she felt there was something sinister in the appearances of the ferrididdles.

Glenn lit the bedroom lamp, then taking Bernice by the hand, he led her from room to room and lit the lamps throughout the house. He also checked the front and back doors and the windows and, as well as he could detect, found there had been no tampering with them. Still neither had any desire to sleep; so Glenn built a wood fire in the fireplace and they sat up the remainder of the night.

By the time daylight came, they had decided to return to Cleveland. They prepared and ate a light breakfast, then began to pack their luggage and load the car. Just as they were about ready to leave, Bernice remembered that she had promised one of their neighbors in Cleveland to get some wild fern fronds for her on this trip. While Glenn made a last minute check about the premises, Bernice went into the woods back of the lodge to get the ferns.

Shortly thereafter, Glenn heard his wife scream. Thinking that she might have seen another ferrididdle, he started out around the house at a leisurely stride; however, when he saw her, he broke into a run toward her. She was standing over knee-deep in a leaf-filled depression and screaming at the top of her voice. As he ran toward her, he noticed she was not looking toward him but was staring at something beside her. Extending upward through the leaves at her side was a man's leg.

Glenn lifted his wife out of the leaves then both ran to

the car and immediately drove to Elkins to notify the authorities. Later, when they returned with the sheriff, the coroner and others and the body was removed from the leaf-filled pit, it was found to be that of Bud Slagle. It appeared he had been clubbed to death.

The murder of Bud Slagle has remained a mystery. Yet, there were some people in the community who were intrigued by this event because of what had occurred only a few miles from there about the same time. A housewife, while at the barn milking the cows early one morning, was attacked and then bludgeoned to death. Her attacker was later found to be an inmate of the Medium Security Prison at nearby Huttonsville who, after murdering the woman, had returned to the prison and gone back to bed. In his subsequent trial, he was found guilty of murder and was executed at the state penitentiary. Although there was no evidence of any connection between these two crimes, it was suspected by some people they were both committed by the same person.

Glenn and Bernice returned to Cleveland and never again visited at Glenbernie Lodge. Sometime thereafter, the lodge was sold to a group of sportsmen but before they had an opportunity to use it, some intruders, through their carelessness, burned it down.

To Judgment Brought

At Low Gap Run in the eastern section of Gilmer County was the farm home of the family of Benjamin Johnson. In the spring of 1858, the time of the incident related here, the family consisted of Ben, his wife, Susan, and a five-year old son, Richard. At the time, Susan was pregnant with a child who, at birth, would be named Mary and destined never to know her father.

Although regarded as a fairly successful farmer with the status of slaveholder, Ben Johnson, at thirty-seven, was not a happy man. Easily provoked to anger and with little compassion for others, he was a man to be feared, especially by his slave, William. Moreover, the independent spirit of William only aggravated Ben's evil nature. Sometimes when William crossed his master, he was tied to a post and lashed with a blacksnake whip across his bare back until the blood ran down and soaked the waistband of his trousers. As additional punishment, Ben, on some occasions, rubbed salt into the cuts and wounds on William's mutilated back.

Because of the nature of slaveholding in Western Virginia at that time, people were somewhat suspicious of the desirability of slaves who were offered for sale. So both times that William was sold to other farmers, the condition of sale was that he could be returned if he proved to be unsatisfactory; and both times he was brought back to the Johnson homestead -- a living hell for him.

Early one morning in June, Ben took William with him to cut weeds in the tobacco patch above the house. Soon after they arrived there and had begun their labor, William suddenly attacked Ben by hitting him several times on the head with his hoe and killing him almost instantly. William then placed Ben's body in a ravine and covered it with leaves and limbs he broke from trees nearby.

Now that he had freed himself from his evil master, William was in a quandary as to what he should do next. After recalling that there was a large wheat field nearby, he cautiously made his way there and hid. When night came, he crept out of his hiding place and went to the Johnson cellar for milk. At first he was careful not to drink very much milk from each crock so it would not be missed by Mrs. Johnson and others at the homestead. However, by the third night he was so famished that he drank most of the contents of one crock before stopping.

The next day high sheriff E. T. Stout was informed of the disappearing milk. When night came, the sheriff and his deputies were hiding about the cellar and, as expected, William came back for more milk. He was promptly captured and placed in the county jail in Glenville.

Although the Supreme Court of the United States had ruled in the Dred Scott case only the year before that slaves were property and therefore not entitled to a court trial, nevertheless, the County Court of Gilmer County decided to grant William a fair trial by that body. The trial began during the July term in 1858 with Philip Cox as presiding justice and William Lynch, Robert Kirkpatrick, James Cather and Moses W. Farnsworth as gentlemen justices.

Gilmer County court records show the following:

Commonwealth vs. William, a slave: felony.

The property of Benjamin Johnson, deceased, of Gilmer County, who stands charged with a felony by him committed in the County of Gilmer, and within the jurisdiction of this court; in this, that he did on the 4th day of June, 1858, willfully, deliberately, premeditatedly kill Benj. Johnson, was this day set; and the attorney for the Commonwealth, as well as Wm. E. Lively, who was by the court appointed counsel for the prisoner, being present at the bar in the custody of the sheriff of this county, and the said slave being thereupon arraigned, pleaded not guilty. And the court having partly heard the evidence and not having time to conclude the same was adjourned until the next morning at eight o'clock, until which time the case is continued and said slave is remanded to jail.

The court opened next morning (July 21) and Levi Johnson was appointed by the court to write down the testimony in the case. Court then adjourned until the following morning. Next day all the evidence was heard; but the court not having time to hear the argument, it adjourned until the next morning at eight o'clock. The court convened next morning . . . and it was ordered by the court that the slave, William, be hanged by the neck until dead. It was further ordered that the sentence upon him be executed publicly on Friday the first day of October, between the hours of ten in the morning and four in the afternoon, on a lot belonging to W. S. Fell, in the hollow above the M. E. Church. Until that time the slave was remanded to jail.

The court proceeded to value the slave as the law directed. Each justice present in the court affixed to him such value as in his opinion the slave would bring if sold publicly under a knowledge of the circumstance of his guilt. Whereupon Philip Cox valued him at $775, William Lynch at $500,

Robert Kirkpatrick at $600, and Moses W. Farnsworth at $700. Upon which the legal value was ascertained to be $635. Robert Linn was at the time prosecuting attorney. William E. Lively, the slave's counsel, was by an order of the court allowed $25 to be paid out of the estate of Benjamin Johnson.

When daylight came on that first day of October in 1858, people could be seen coming into Glenville from all directions -- some on horseback, some in wagons and buggies, and many on foot. Most of them brought their lunches with them and came prepared to spend the entire day in the village. The scaffold for the execution had been erected in the lower part of the ravine above the M.E. Church and directly behind the present location of Pickens Hall of Glenville State College. As the people arrived in town, they immediately congregated in the area round about the scaffold until every available foot of ground within sight of the scaffold was occupied.

About two o'clock in the afternoon, William, the convicted slave, was removed from the jail back of the court house and hurriedly brought across to the scaffold. With his hands tied behind him, he was helped up the stairway onto the platform where he, almost immediately, in a loud, yet calm, voice, delivered a long and moving prayer. Then in a clear, tremulous voice he sang the song that had seemed to comfort him during his long hours in prison, "Must I Be to Judgment Brought to Answer in that Day?" At the conclusion of his song, the noose was adjusted around his neck and a black hood put over his head. Shortly thereafter, Sheriff E.T. Stout sprang the trap and William plunged through the opening in the platform; his body jerked spasmodically a few times and then hung lifeless.

The reaction of the crowd to William's performance and

his ensuing execution was mixed. While some stared in stony silence throughout the proceedings, others openly and unashamedly wept. There were many who believed that the crime committed by William, though an abhorrent one, was justifiable in his situation.

Following the hanging, the sheriff took charge of the body and had it removed to the county poor farm for burial. His grave is said to be located near the seventh putting green on the Glenville Golf Course.

The Apparition
on Court House Square

When Uncle Pete Kelly sat down beside the white-haired old gentleman on a bench at the Court House Square on that warm spring morning in 1897, little did he realize what a bizarre experience was in store for him. During the course of a casual conversation with the aged man, Uncle saw, some forty feet distant at another bench, a man who bore a remarkable resemblance to the one who sat beside him. Noting Pete's observation, the man beside him nodded his head in the direction of the other and said, "That is Doug Graham. He is no longer with us; his unfortunate ordeal made an old man of him overnight and all before his twenty-fifth birthday." Then, in a low voice and completely devoid of any show of empathy, the aged man recounted to my uncle the events in Doug Graham's life which destroyed him.

Doug's father, Alec, was a farmer and livestock dealer. Each year in late fall, he, with his drovers, took a herd of cattle by way of the dusty turnpike to an Eastern market. Because of the presence of highwaymen waiting to relieve him of his money from the sale of the cattle, he knew he had to take special care on the way back home. Also, because of the scarcity of banks he had to keep his money at home under a guard maintained night and day for weeks after his return.

One fall Alec and his drovers set out once more on the long drive to market. Seventeen-year-old Doug was left at home with his invalid mother to manage the farm during his father's absence and to be on guard against those who might lie in wait for his father at the homestead.

About ten days after Alec left home, Doug began his night watch, even though he did not expect his father to return until four or five days later. This night was dark except for occasional breaks of light from a full moon that raced through dark, billowy clouds. During one such interval of light, Doug saw something move behind the grape vines at the backyard fence. Intensely alert now, he waited for the light to return. Although the next light span was only momentary, he was able to see a man skulking there. Taking careful aim with his rifle, he fired into the vines where the man had stood. On finding that he had killed the prowler, he then dragged the body to a far corner of the barn lot and covered it with some discarded fence posts.

Night after night Doug continued his watch. The time for his father's return came and passed, but still no alarm was felt because on other occasions he had been delayed. But after three weeks had passed, some anxiety was felt for his safety. Adding to the distress of the family was a vicious rumor that perhaps he had not intended to come back.

Weeks grew into months and months into years without a happy reunion at the Graham home. Doug's secret of the murder was well concealed and he tried to settle it with his own conscience as being a justifiable act of defense of his home.

Following his mother's demise, he continued to live at the old homestead alone. One quiet night, he was awakened by the chilling cry of a screech owl as it flew over the bedroom corner of the house. Then from a distance came the sound of running feet, growing ever louder and closer and suddenly, with heavy stomping, it crossed the full length of the front porch and continued with gradually diminishing noise in the direction of the barnyard. After this had occurred on several different nights, Doug began to suspect it to be the ghost of the man he had slain.

Then on a calm afternoon the shutters on all the windows of the house flew open and banged shut repeatedly as if in a violent storm. At another time, with shocking suddenness, a fence post came crashing through his bedroom window, shattering the stillness of the night.

On the edge of the community at the head of a dark hollow there lived a wrinkled old recluse by the name of Granny Neff. She was widely known for her eccentric way of living and was said to consort with witches and ghosts. In desperation Doug went to her for advice. Between puffs on her gray clay pipe and with her piercing black eyes studying him, she said: "Young man, you've got a guilty conscience. That ghost is trying to tell you something."

Doug believed he already knew what the ghost was trying to tell him. He forced himself to go to the barn lot and to the pile of decaying posts under which he had hidden the body. On removing the posts he found a skeleton lying there and dangling from a rib on a chain was a large pocket watch. Recognition was instantaneous. Covering his face with his hands, he cried out in anguish: "Oh, my God, what have I done!"

The sudden realization that he had mistakenly slain his father was more than he could bear. His traumatic experience made a white-haired old man of him overnight and never again was he able to walk alone.

Soon after the story was concluded, a man with a wheelchair approached. "Well, Graham, old fellow," he said to the storyteller, "it's time to go back over the bridge." The aged man was gently helped into the vehicle. As they departed, on the back of the wheelchair could be seen in bold, black letters the words: PROPERTY OF STATE ASYLUM FOR THE INSANE.

On looking back to the bench where the subject of the old man's story had sat, Uncle saw that he, too, had departed. Wishing to learn more about Doug Graham, he inquired among others who were closer to where that person had been a few moments before. Not only was he unable to learn more about the man, he could find no one who had even seen him there.

A China Doll

The decade of the 1880's marked a turning point in the history of southern West Virginia. Prior to that time practically all of the people residing in that area were of Anglo-Saxon or Scotch-Irish lineage whose ancestors had migrated into this region in the late eighteenth and early nineteenth centuries. They were an independent and stalwart people who were often poor in worldly goods, yet were generally content with their lot and proud of their heritage.

Then came Frederick Kimball's "act of imagination" that changed the course of the history of that area -- the extension of the Norfolk and Western Railroad into this fabulously rich Pocahontas coal field. An immediate result was the influx of new people whose way of life often clashed with that of the native stock. Generally, the newcomers were looked upon by the native people as inferior interlopers. Moreover, the superstitious hill people considered the subterranean occupation of coal mining to be unlucky as well as demeaning and only a little less than peonage. Farming, timbering, and even whiskey-making (then claimed by some of the natives as a constitutionally guaranteed right) were regarded as being superior to coal digging and loading.

Among the newcomers was Tony Borro whose tall, hulking frame and pock-marked face from an earlier bout with smallpox gave him a sinister appearance. After a short stint as a miner he, through some maneuvering the native people never understood, became the chief of police in Aracoma. After only a brief tenure in his new position he had shot two men, allegedly in self-defense, was regarded as trigger-happy and basically a coward. For some of the out-of-town native people, the "good old days" of coming to town on Saturdays for a time of greeting and drinking, and sometimes wrangling, with old friends were not the same, thanks to the ubiquitous Borro.

About two miles back on a mountain from Aracoma lived Big Red Naylor with his wife, Sarah, and children Tom and Selma. He had a small farm on which he raised fruits, especially peaches, corn and a few vegetables. As a quiet sideline, he made peach brandy and "corn likker" for which he found a ready market, along with his produce, in Aracoma. In the summer and fall of the year Big Red would often be seen driving his decrepit one-horse wagon about town making deliveries.

When sober, Big Red was a jovial man, kind and gentle to his wife and children; but when he became drunk, he was cruel, downright mean and unpredictable. His son, Tom, at the age of eleven, seemed to know how to avoid any confrontation with his father; however, little Selma, seven years old, was often the object of his anger when he was drunk and quaked with fear of her father. On his becoming sober, he would apologize for his actions and little Selma would laugh nervously -- a laugh that was coarse and hollow and devoid of mirth.

One warm summer day after Big Red had made his deliveries in Aracoma, he was in a jovial mood as he and his son, Tom, were leaving town. While crossing the Guyandotte River bridge and singing in a loud and boisterous manner, he was stopped by Borro who gave him a tongue-lashing for disturbing the peace. When Big Red talked back,

Borro hopped up in the wagon and pistol-whipped him until he was unconscious. Borro then told Tom to tell his father, when he revived, not to come back to town again.

On his regaining consciousness, Big Red seethed with anger and began to drink heavily. By the time they reached home he was in a very nasty mood. When Selma saw her drunken father coming, she huddled behind a chair on the front porch with her china doll cuddled in her arms. Big Red staggered onto the porch, knocked the chair aside, snatched the doll from Selma and hurled it to the floor. He then stormed into the house while his daughter remained there in stunned silence. At her feet lay her broken china doll.

The next day Big Red was sober and penitent.

"I'm sorry I broke your doll, Selma," he said to her.

"That's all right, Daddy," Selma replied, then began to laugh nervously.

When Big Red put his hand gently on Selma's head and drew her closer to him, her laughing turned to crying; then burying her face against his shoulder, she sobbed as if her heart would break.

"Now, now, Babe," he said in a husky voice. "I don't suppose they've stopped making china dolls."

A few days later Big Red, in defiance of the order of Chief Borro to stay out of town, strode boldly into Aracoma. He was sober, alert and outwardly calm; inside, he seethed with anger.

Later in the day as he emerged from a store, he saw Borro standing in the street and looking directly at him. As Big Red moved his right hand toward his coat pocket, Borro drew his gun and shot him. Big Red came tumbling down the steps of the store building and rolled into the street where he lay still.

As the people crowded round, Borro said: "You saw

him reach for his gun, didn't you? I had to shoot him."

A friend of Big Red leaned over him and lifted his hand from his pocket. It was not a gun he clasped in his hand, but a china doll.

The hatred of the people toward Borro became so intense he left Aracoma immediately and was never seen there again. In the meantime, Big Red's wife was notified of his death. When Sarah and her children came to town to remove the body, they scorned the proffered help of bystanders and managed to get Big Red in the wagon by themselves. Before leaving town, Sarah purchased some black cloth and pine boards with which to make a coffin and placed them in the wagon beside the body.

As they rode along toward home, Tom drove while Selma sat, dry-eyed and calm, beside her mother.

"Your Daddy did love you, Selma," Sarah said gently. "Just getting another doll for you the way he did took a lot of courage. He really did love you."

Selma looked straight ahead and did not reply.

Late on the night of the wake when all the guests were in the kitchen, Selma brought her broken doll to the coffin. After giving it a gentle hug and a kiss, she placed it in the coffin beside her father's body. As noiselessly as she had come, she crept back to her bed and quietly cried herself to sleep.

Invasion of the Green Monsters

Late in the evening of September 13, 1952, a number of unidentified spacecraft passed over the eastern area of the United States. They were moving in a north-westward direction and were observed by people in Virginia, Maryland, Pennsylvania and Ohio as well as in West Virginia. While passing over the Allegheny Plateau, at least three of the spacecraft became separated from the others, two of which apparently met with disaster in the hills of Clay and Braxton Counties of West Virginia. Whether these were remote control destructions or accidental ones, no one here will ever know. However, a review of the evidence as reported by those who witnessed the strange happenings indicates that both causes may have been involved.

In Clay County a number of witnesses reported having observed a strange luminous ball passing low overhead in the twilight of the evening. On its drifting to a lower elevation, it ended in a dazzling flash of light on a wooded hillside. Those who investigated the scene soon afterward reported that the spacecraft, while on the way to obliteration against the hill, had seared a swath of forest foliage crisp and brown, and filled the air thereabouts with a lingering acrid odor.

The incident which received the most widespread publicity was the appearance of the so-called "Braxton County Green Monster." Mrs. Kathleen May of Flatwoods, a few days after the occurrence, reported to a nationwide television audience that she joined a group of young people to investigate the claim of her two sons that they had seen a flying saucer land on the hillside overlooking the small town. On climbing the hill they "came upon a monster ten feet tall, with a bright green body and a blood-red face" which moved toward them with a sliding, floating motion. A noxious odor filled the area which brought on violent choking spasms and vomiting by some members of the search party as they fled from the scene. Subsequently, investigators reported smelling the sickening odor as well as observing burnt and broken branches of the trees where the flying object had landed, but the monster and its spacecraft had disappeared.

An incident which received little publicity at the time was that observed on the same evening by George Snitowsky and his wife, Edith, of Queens, New York, while they were traveling by car between Frametown and Gassaway, a few miles to the east of Flatwoods. Without any forewarning, the motor of their car stopped and a quick check indicated that the practically new battery was dead. They said that suddenly a faintly sickening odor somewhat like a mixture of burnt sulphur and ether filled the air about them and caused their baby to have an attack of coughing and gagging. While Edith attempted to console the child, George went out to try to locate the source of the odor.

Crossing over a slight rise to the left of the highway, he saw, some sixty yards down the slope, a large spheroid moving slowly back and forth as it hovered near the ground and from it came a soft, violet light. On moving closer to the object, he felt the sensation of thousands of needle-like vibrations irritating the skin of his whole body. Nauseated, he turned and stumbled back toward the car.

From the car Edith gave a piercing scream. George could

see her ashen face, her trembling lips, and her eyes wide and staring.

"Edith, for God's sake, what's the matter?" George shouted.

"Hurry, George, hurry," she cried in terror. "It's coming behind you!"

George glanced back over his shoulder and saw, some thirty feet behind him, a figure about eight or nine feet tall with a big head, bloated body, and long, spindly arms gliding rapidly toward him. On entering the car he hurriedly ran up the windows, locked the doors, then dived to the floor under the steering column. Meanwhile, Edith had crouched with the baby to the floor in the back seat of the car where she tried to relieve her child of its gagging and crying by placing a silk handkerchief over its face. Then, terror-stricken, they waited to see what the monster would do.

After some time, George rose up slowly and saw a long, spindly arm, forked into two soft ends, reach across the windshield and touch the hood of the car. After another agonizing wait, he looked again and saw the monster glide across the road and up and over the slope in the direction of its spacecraft. With a feeling of slight relief they watched and waited.

"Then," George related later, "my eye caught sight of the ascending irridescent globe over the trees. . . . It rose slowly and made intermittent stops, hanging in mid-air for a split second before continuing upward. And then at about three thousand feet, I guess, it swung back and forth like a pendulum gathering momentum. Suddenly it swooped up in an elliptical arc and with a dazzling trail of light, shot completely out of sight."

A half-hour later the Snitowskys, pale-faced and still thoroughly shaken from the ordeal, stopped at a motel in

Sutton for the night without telling anyone at the time about their terrifying experience. Because of the usual skepticism held by the public toward such phenomena and the accompanying ridicule for those reporting having seen them, they believed it wise, for the time, to remain silent.

The next morning while getting gas at a nearby service station before resuming their trip, the attendant pointed out to Snitowsky a V-shaped brown spot on the hood of his car that appeared to have been burned into the paint. Having heard of the Flatwoods scare of the evening before, the attendant said in mock seriousness: "It looks as if the Green Monster was after you, too."

Looking the attendant directly in the eye, George replied: "I wish you could have seen it."

As the family drove away, the attendant said to his helper: "By golly, he said that as if he really meant it!"

Spirits of White Lightning

Because of an Anglo-Saxon-Celtic cultural heritage, a constant struggle with an unkind environment, a restricted social outlet, and a fierce pride in their freedom, some Southern Appalachian people have found it ever agreeable with their own conscience to engage in the production of stimulating beverages unrestrained. For many years it was a legitimate and common activity and regarded by some as a necessity for their livelihood. Thus, when the yet young federal government placed an excise tax on whiskey production, the people of the Alleghenies refused to pay it. They saw this tax as a violation of their constitutional rights. Even after the tax was removed from the smallest distillers a year later, the mountain people's opposition continued and culminated in a rebellion against the federal government. Although the rebellion was easily quelled, the continued distaste for the excise tax law brought about its early repeal.

The law requiring a person to have a license to make and retail intoxicating beverages was ignored by many mountain people. As a result, literally hundreds of illicit distillers in Western Virginia were caught and prosecuted during the early part of the nineteenth century. With the coming of the Civil War, the federal government again put a tax on domestic liquors as a means to help finance that war. Nevertheless, some people continued to operate "moonshine stills" in secluded spots in defiance of laws they could not accept.

Intermittently, for more than a century there has been a struggle going on in Southern Appalachia between government revenue agents or other authorities and the illegal distillers. In this period of time the product of their endeavors has assumed a variety of names, the most commonly known ones being "moonshine", "home brew", "mountain dew", and "white lightning." Perhaps the "white lightning" term best describes the clear liquid beverage and its potency.

In this long struggle, whenever a "moonshiner" was apprehended by the authorities and sent to prison for a course in basketmaking or weaving chair bottoms, it usually taught him little; his release from prison was often followed by the setting up of a new distillery, or "still", under more elaborate precautionary measures.

One story that is well known throughout Appalachia is about a revenue agent who went into the mountains in search of a particular moonshiner. Although the hill people have long been known for their friendly attitude and helpfulness to others, they can also be reticent and cool toward suspicious outlanders. So, as the revenue agent searched for the illegal distiller, he was often thwarted in his efforts by being given the "silent treatment" or outright misinformation.

In time, however, the agent arrived at the mountaineer's cabin and was met at the front door by a small, sharp-eyed boy. When the agent asked to speak to the boy's father, the boy replied: "He ain't here."

"Could you tell me where he is?" the agent inquired.

"Yep."

"Well, where is he?"

"He's up in the woods makin'," the boy answered.

"Could I speak to your mother, then?" the agent asked.

"No."

"Why not?"

"'Cause she ain't here."

"Could you tell me where she is?"

"Yep."

"Well?"

"She's up in the woods makin', too," the boy finally admitted.

The agent then offered to pay the boy fifty cents if he would show him the way to his father. As an answer to the agent's offer, the boy held out his open hand.

"You'll have to take me up there first," the agent stated flatly. "I'll pay you when we get back."

"I'll take the money now," the boy said evenly, "'cause you ain't comin' back."

Heady Revenge

At the time of the beginning of the Civil War, John Jennings lived with his wife and their two small sons, Frank and Jack, on a farm in Wetzel County. Only a few years prior to this, he had bought the farm which was located between Doolin and Fishing Creeks about three miles from New Martinsville. Most of the people in that area at the time were strongly for the Union and some military units were being formed of volunteers thereabouts. In a spontaneous act of patriotism, John Jennings joined a company of volunteers which, soon thereafter, was accepted into the Union Army.

After being away from home a few months, John became so homesick to see his wife and children he could think of little else day or night. His worry about his family and loss of sleep began to sap his strength and affect the performance of his duties. If he could only be with his family a short time, he thought, he could settle down and do a much better job of soldiering. When he approached his commanding officer with a request for a brief leave to visit his family, he was perfunctorily dismissed. The time came when he could stand it no longer, so he deserted his company and returned home.

Word was soon spread about the community that John Jennings was back home with his family and immediately some members of the "home guards" went out to investigate. When John saw them coming, he suddenly had visions of being court martialed and possibly executed for desertion from the Army. He at once started running towards the woods back of the house; the "home guards" followed him in close pursuit, but he escaped.

Over the next several months John lived much of the time in caves in the woods with occasional brief visits to his home. It usually occurred that whenever he did come back to his house, the "guards" heard about it and in their efforts to capture him, they scared him away again. A number of times his wife had to take supplies to him in the woods because it was thought to be unsafe for him to venture out of hiding. As a result of one such trip on a bitter cold winter night, she suffered so much from exposure she was stricken with pneumonia fever and died.

When John heard that President Lincoln had issued an offer of pardon to all deserters who immediately returned to their military posts, he first made arrangements for his sons to be taken care of, then he rejoined his military unit. On his arrival back in camp, his former buddies completely ignored him. He was shunned as if he were a leper; he had to mess and pitch his tent apart from them from the time of his re-entry into the service until the war ended.

When the men of John's company were discharged and put aboard a ship to be returned home, he was forcibly put off the ship by his former buddies and had to find a way home on his own. His arrival home, as he expected, was not a happy event for him. His children were glad to see him, but most of his neighbors and former friends treated him as if he were an outlaw.

After some time, John remarried and tried to establish a normal life in the community with his second wife and Frank and Jack, the sons of his first marriage. Although he enjoyed a congenial home life, elsewhere he was not permitted to forget his past. While his sons were growing to manhood, they became extremely embittered over the treatment their father received. By the time they were late teenagers, they had decided to seek revenge on all those who had persecuted their father in any way, even though he begged them to ignore what had happened.

Soon after Frank and Jack began to rob and steal from some of their father's persecutors, they were joined in their activities by a number of ex-convicts, fugitives from justice and young delinquents. The gang's activities were extended to highway robbery, rapine and attempted murder and brought on a reign of terror in the hills of Wetzel County.

The residents of the area lived in a constant state of anxiety and fear. People who had formerly left their doors and windows open on hot summer nights, now closed and locked them out of fear of the Jennings gang. There were many rumors circulated about evil doings of the gang which never occurred yet these added to the disrepute that tarnished the former good name of the county.

The real and imagined doings of the gang seemed to defy all efforts of the local authorities to restrain. It reached a point where it could no longer be tolerated so the people decided to take action. In 1873, several men organized an extra-legal, clandestine group known as the Red Men. They wore uniforms with pillow-case style head coverings made of red cloth. Usually in a quiet, orderly movement, they visited the homes of those persons who had befriended members of the Jennings gang, ordered the families to leave the county and then promptly burned their houses down. Within a short time, a number of blackened home sites dotted the countryside.

About two o'clock one night the Red Men appeared at the home of John Jennings. He must have been expecting them to come because, even though the night was unusually warm, they found him in bed fully dressed. The Red Men were not there to punish him, because they knew he had opposed his sons' illegal activities, but had come to get information on his sons' whereabouts. When he informed them he had no idea where they were, the men asked him to go with them. He was being held, they informed him, until his sons were found.

When John refused to go along with the Red Men, they tried to put a rope around him, but he struggled free. Meanwhile, John's wife, thinking the men were going to kill her husband, ran to the woodyard for an axe and brought it to him. The men then opened fire, killing John immediately and slightly wounding his wife.

As soon as Frank and Jack Jennings learned of their father's death, they fled from the county and were never seen there again. However, some people claimed that the spirits of these men were known to roam the hills of Wetzel County for several years thereafter. Fox-hunters out on moonlit nights often reported seeing fleeting specters in silhouette as they moved along the crests of Flinderation and Doolin Ridges. Those who saw the ghostly shadows speculated that the evil deeds perpetrated by the Jennings brothers were so wicked that the souls of those men were not permitted any rest until some retribution had been made.

Twins in the Whirlpool

On the south bank of the Little Kanawha River near its mouth was a tavern known as The Rest. Near its front entrance there was a swinging sign on which were the words "Entertainment for Man and Beast." From the time of its being licensed to serve the public as a tavern in 1789 until it went out of business in 1850, it served as a temporary stoping place for countless numbers of restless pioneers on the march westward. The local settlers of the area also met there and related tales of Indian fighting, of struggles they had with bears and panthers, and about the lusty life of boating and rafting on the river. Here, too, some came to learn the latest news from passing travelers as well as to discuss the leading questions of the day.

One item of discussion that aroused considerable interest for some time was about the activities of the George Lemon family. Some of the habitues of The Rest well remembered the day George first arrived on the Little Kanawha. Somewhat to their surprise was his announcement that he had come up from lower Virginia to develop a commercial salt works in the vicinity. Although the Great Kanawha River Valley was widely known for its salt deposits, the only salt brine location of any significance along the Little Kanawha was at Bulltown, a hundred miles up river. So it was with more than usual interest that the people there followed the activities of the Lemons.

Soon after George had chosen a house site for his family at the forks of the Hughes River, a tributary of the Little Kanawha, he became aware of the presence of oil floating on the water that flowed past his residence. Visualizing the possibilities of a profitable part-time sideline to the salt business he hoped to establish, George at once began to make plans to trap the oil. Since it was in the fall of the year when the river was at low stage, he put his sons to the task of digging pits in the sand of the river channel. As the oil seeped into these pits, it was collected and stored in barrels to await shipment to market.

One day the people at The Rest saw a log raft coming down the Little Kanawha, the first of many such rafts of its kind that were to follow in subsequent years. On this raft were George Lemon and one of his sons with a cargo of oil. At the junction of the Little Kanawha with the Ohio, the barrels of oil were transferred from the raft to a steamboat while the raft was sold to the proprietors of a local sawmill. From that point the steamboat transported the oil up river to Marietta where it was sold to the firm of Bosworth, Wells and Company for thirty-three cents a gallon. This firm, in turn, sold the oil to drug and chemical companies in Pittsburgh, Baltimore, Cincinnati, New York and St. Louis under the label of "Seneca Oil." It was regarded as having rare medicinal properties for the treatment of ailments of both man and beast. One of the more common uses of the oil was its application to harness-worn sores on draft animals.

When George and his sons eventually got back to their initial interest and sank a well in quest of salt brine, they only found more oil. This new discovery drew considerable attention to the area. One person who was especially interested was Bushrod Creel. He successfully claimed ownership of this land and soon replaced the Lemons in the production of oil.

Late one evening two husky teenaged boys arrived at The Rest. They were Otho and Argil Boston, twin sons of the widow Boston of Belpre. They had heard about the new oil business on the Hughes River and were hoping to find employment there.

Before leaving home, the boys had spent many long hours trying to convince their mother that they were old enough to work away from home. Because the boys' father had lost his life in a steam boiler explosion on the Ohio, she did not want her sons to work on the river. After promising their mother they would not seek work on steamboats, the twins were granted permission to look for employment elsewhere.

While at the tavern, the twins met Bushrod Creel who agreed to hire them as apprentices. On the following morning it was with considerable excitement they set out with their new employer for the oil works on the Hughes River. They were especially pleased over the fact they would not be separated in their employment; they could not remember ever being apart from each other, even for a day.

After working there for some time in a variety of jobs, the brothers were then assigned to help operate a raft in the transportation of the oil down river to Parkersburg. They talked this over between themselves and jointly concluded that working on a raft would not violate the promise they had made to their mother not to work on steamboats. They saw this, too, as an opportunity to visit with their mother more often.

Early one morning a raft laden with several barrels of oil was untied from its mooring at the Creel oil works. In charge of the craft were Abe Pack, an experienced riverman, and the Boston twins. As they drifted down the placid Hughes River, they had no way of knowing of the perils that awaited them.

At that time the Little Kanawha River above its junction with the Hughes was rapidly nearing flood stage even though there had been only a light rain in the Hughes River area. Some cloudbursts farther up the Little Kanawha had turned the normally clear and calm little river into a turbid, whirling torrent. While still some distance from the junction of the two rivers, Abe at first detected a slowing down of the raft. Some distance farther down he noticed that the river had come to a standstill. Shortly thereafter, the raft began to drift back upstream. Realizing there was something amiss on the Little Kanawha, he directed the twins to help him maneuver the raft closer to the river bank where they tied it to a nearby tree. There they waited until much of the flood water of the Little Kanawha had moved on.

Then believing it safe to venture out again, Abe and the twins guided the raft with its cargo of oil out into midstream and at once began moving slowly down river. The backup water from the Little Kanawha had subsided and the Hughes appeared to be near normal again.

On their entering the water of the Little Kanawha, they saw the banks of that stream still littered with debris left by the flood. The water was muddy and still above the normal stage of flow. They noticed, too, as they moved downstream, that uprooted trees and logs occasionally blocked portions of the channel and only through skillful maneuvering of the raft were they able to avoid them.

Abe's long experience on the river had taught him to keep a constant lookout for whirlpools, and with special precaution during and immediately after floods. Just as the Indian name of the Great Kanawha meant "river of whirlpools", it could, likewise, have been applied to the Little Kanawha as well.

Some eight or ten miles below the mouth of the Hughes

River, the channel of the Little Kanawha became somewhat narrower. As they approached that location, Abe detected the presence of a whirlpool at the right side of the river. Believing there was ample space to pass through safely on the left, he instructed the twins to help him steer the raft in that direction. Near the surface of the water on the left side, yet not visible to the occupants on the raft, was a huge log directly in their path.

When the raft ran against the sunken log, the force of the collision threw Abe headlong into the smooth-flowing side of the river, while the raft, with the twins still on board, swung sharply sideways and directly into the path of the whirlpool. The twins in their fright could only cling together in sheer terror. Suddenly, the raft capsized and the twins disappeared into the swirling vortex of the whirlpool. After Abe had clambered up the south bank of the river to a place of safety, he looked back and saw only logs and barrels scattered over the river; the twins were nowhere to be seen.

In all subsequent searches, the bodies of the twins were never found. After several weeks had passed, Mrs. Boston, accompanied by a close friend, rode up from Belpre by way of the newly constructed Staunton Turnpike to view the place where her sons had last been seen. While she and her friend stood there on the bank and looked down into the river, what appeared to be an arm rose up out of the water and waved them back from the danger spot. Then as the mother looked down into the whirlpool's foamy vortex, she was sure she saw, for one fleeting moment, the pallid, terror-stricken faces of her sons.

In the years that followed, even after a subsequent flood had washed the whirlpool out, rivermen stopping at The Rest often reported they had heard strange noises as they passed the location of the mishap. Some believed the place was haunted; it seemed to be habitually visited by the restless spirits of the unfortunate twins.